LANDMINES

IN THE PATH OF THE BELIEVER

DR. CHARLES F. STANLEY

THOMAS NELSON
Since 1798

NASHVILLE   DALLAS   MEXICO CITY   RIO DE JANEIRO   BEIJING

Published in Nashville, Tennessee, by Thomas Nelson, Inc.

Nelson Books titles may be purchased in bulk for educational, business, fund-raising, or sales promotional use. For information, please email SpecialMarkets@ThomasNelson.com.

Unless otherwise noted, Scripture quotations are from the NEW AMERICAN STANDARD BIBLE®, © Copyright The Lockman Foundation 1960, 1962, 1963, 1968, 1971, 1972, 1973, 1975, 1977, 1995. Used by permission.

Scripture quotations noted NIV are from the HOLY BIBLE: NEW INTERNATIONAL VERSION®. Copyright © 1973, 1978, 1984 by International Bible Society. Used by permission of Zondervan. All rights reserved.

Page design by Walter Petrie.

Library of Congress Cataloging-in-Publication Data

Stanley, Charles F.
    Landmines in the path of the believer / Charles F. Stanley.
      p. cm.
    ISBN-13: 978-1-4002-0090-0 (hardcover)
    ISBN-10: 1-4002-0090-3 (hardcover)
    1. Christian life. 2. Spiritual warfare. I. Title.
BV4501.3.S7335 2007
248.4—dc22   2007018650

Printed in the United States of America

07 08 09 10 11 QW 5 4 3 2 1

*This book is dedicated to the Board Members
of In Touch Ministries*

*— Dean Hancock, Ben Reed, Maurice Templeton,
and Steve Yungerberg —*

for their faithful and loyal support in helping us reach

the world with the glorious message of Christ.

No temptation has overtaken you

but such as is common to man;

and God is faithful,

who will not allow you to be tempted

beyond what you are able,

but with the temptation

will provide the way of escape also,

so that you will be able to endure it.

—1 CORINTHIANS 10:13

CONTENTS

INTRODUCTION

Over the years, men and women have died so that we could have the freedom we enjoy today. Most of us have known someone who has served our country in the armed forces. I've often listened as men have talked about their experiences and wondered what it felt like for them to face severe enemy threat.

It doesn't take long to realize that when you are in the heat of the battle, the enemy will do anything to bring you down in defeat. This is especially true on physical battlefields, but also on the spiritual front lines where Satan lurks—seeking to destroy us so we will not serve God or do His will.

If you have accepted Jesus Christ as your Savior, then you need to know that the enemy will stop at nothing to prevent you from knowing God and living for Jesus Christ. He does this by creating a major conflict across the landscape of your life. Extreme as it may seem, Satan is convinced that if he can accomplish his wretched goals, you will become discouraged and fearful, and you will want to give up. A disarmed, discouraged believer who has fallen into the dust of defeat, suffocated by guilt and shame, is no threat to him. Be aware: he does not hesitate to use extreme tactics of warfare—ones that are specifically designed to separate you from God and His blessings, as well as the love and respect of friends and family.

THE TRUTH CONCERNING LANDMINES

Many people mistakenly think that Satan uses obvious means to draw us off course. However, his most devastating weapons of warfare are barely visible. They lay hidden below the surface of our spiritual landscape. Yet when we move in their direction, they explode beneath us, inflicting deep heartache, sorrow, and brokenness. Sometimes the injury seems beyond repair, but it never is when God is involved.

Over the past few years, we have learned about the powerful brute force of one of the most devastating weapons of warfare—a landmine. A short time ago, many of us never would have thought to list this device as one of the most destructive on a battlefield, but it is. When a veteran speaks of going to war, our minds immediately fill with images of agile aircraft flying at top speed, combat troops outfitted with the latest technology for battle, and tanks—not the kind that once rolled noisily over the landscape of foreign countries, but fast-moving fortresses built to penetrate enemy lines and conquer advancing adversaries.

It is hard to imagine a single piece of metal, which may be no larger than two feet by two feet, having the ability to destroy such military might, but this is exactly what a landmine does. It annihilates whatever is nearby, and the slightest pressure can detonate it.

By the time a landmine is uncovered, it is usually too late to get out of the way. When I think about this, I am reminded why this weapon of warfare is so effective. Its stealthy appearance is sinister and deadly. Just as there are physical landmines placed along pathways and roadsides and out in open fields, Satan strategically places landmines in the path of every believer. There is no such thing as a clear, straight path without landmines. Each day, we face the threat of stepping on a spiritual landmine and suffering the sorrow and devastation this brings.

When we step on one of the enemy's landmines, the explosion that follows usually has an adverse effect on our relationships with God and with others, as well as our personal testimony. It also alters the way we operate in life. We miss out on the joy of experiencing God's richest blessings. We need to make a clear distinction between the landmines on a real battlefield and the ones that Satan plants along our way. They explode beneath us as a result of our fallen world. Others are landmines that the enemy strategically places with an express desire to inflict deep harm on us as believers. If we are not sensitive to the Lord's warning, we can get off course and confront destruction.

YOU DON'T HAVE TO BE A CASUALTY

I have watched people deal with the landmines of life, and their experience ends in one of two ways: either there is spiritual victory and the person grows closer to the Lord, or he is tripped up by Satan's deception and begins a downward spiral that leads to feelings of regret, sorrow, anger, frustration, and—if left unchecked—depression. But you do not have to fall victim to Satan's ploys. Although physical landmines may be hard to spot, God will give you the ability to uncover and disarm the spiritual landmines the enemy has laid across your path. You may feel as though you are standing in a minefield and you do not know which way to turn. I want to assure you that God knows. He has a plan for your rescue. No matter how great the temptation, you can take back any spiritual ground you have given to the enemy and reclaim your rightful position as a child of God.

Peter admonished us to "be of sober spirit, be on the alert. Your adversary, the devil, prowls around like a roaring lion, seeking someone to devour" (1 Peter 5:8). The apostle Paul reminded us that "it was for freedom that Christ set us free; therefore keep standing firm and do not be subject again to a yoke of slavery" (Gal. 5:1). By that he meant being bound by anything that would prevent us from being all that God has planned for us to be. He went on to say, "You were called to freedom . . . do not turn your freedom into an opportunity for the flesh, but through love serve one another" (v. 13).

How do you detect the deadly landmines Satan sets along your roadways, out in open fields where you like to walk, and in hidden locations that you may seldom think of frequenting? My prayer is that as you read this book, God will show you how to uncover and then protect yourself from the enemy's destructive weapons, such as pride, jealousy, feelings of insecurity, sexual sin, disappointment, unforgiveness, compromise, and more. Throughout this study, you also will be given key principles that can help you discover how to live a victorious Christian life without compromising what you know God has given you to do.

Jesus told His disciples, "If you continue in My word, then you are truly disciples of Mine; and you will know the truth, and the truth will make you free" (John 8:31–32). The one thing that exposes, unearths, and disarms any landmine left in the path of a believer is truth—God's truth. When we can practice the principles written in His Word, we experience true freedom from sin, shame, and guilt. This is my prayer for you and all who read this book—that you will learn how to live free of sin's entanglement and reach your full potential as a child of God.

ONE

FACING THE HIDDEN THREAT

King Saul looked across his tent into the eyes of David. It was the first time he had truly stopped to look at the lad, and from his perspective that was exactly what David was: a lad—a youthful man—one who was ruddy in complexion, possibly full of overrated zeal, and looking for his first real chance to prove that he was a first-class warrior. He had come to the right place—the battlefield—a place of strategic warfare.

David was forthright in the king's presence. His résumé included victories over a lion and a bear in defense of his father's flock of sheep. However, Saul knew he would need something more if he planned to emerge the victor from this battle. David's fearless spirit and undaunted desire to avenge God's people caught Saul's attention (1 Sam. 17).

The king relented. David fought Goliath. The rest is history. However, Saul's decision to allow David to fight the Philistine giant was one he would live to regret. This victory became a defining moment in the history of the nation of Israel because it subtly announced the coming of Saul's successor and the end of his reign.

David was greeted in the city streets with celebration: "Saul has slain his thousands, and David his ten thousands" (1 Sam. 18:7). The Bible tells us that from that time, "Saul looked at David with suspicion" (v. 9). Jealousy, pride, and anger filled the king's heart, and David became the target of Saul's personal rage.

FACE-TO-FACE WITH OUR ENEMY

Those who have fought the good fight of faith will tell you that when you are in the heat of a spiritual battle, it does not take long to realize Satan will do anything to prevent you from becoming the person God has planned for you to be. The enemy is a cunning force that you must face. His strategic plan is laid out to entice you to sin and drift in your devotion to God. How does he do this? Satan uses many of the things we feel are harmless or unavoidable sins—gossip, feelings of unforgiveness, pride, and cynicism, to name a few. He also watches to see how we will react to a situation. If there is an opportunity for him to weave his evil mischief into our thoughts, he will take it. This tactic is foundational to his work of laying landmines across our paths. This is especially true on the spiritual front lines of battle where the enemy hides landmines with the intent of using them for our destruction.

The landmines in his arsenal include such sins as pride, jealousy and envy, disappointment, unforgiveness, compromise, sexual temptation, fear, and laziness—which God also calls slothfulness. Each one is designed by Satan to discourage you and keep you from reaching your full potential. That happened in Saul's life. He never fully became the person God created him to be because he allowed pride to enter his heart. If we are not discerning and wise, the same will be true of us.

Yet it may not be pride that creates havoc in our hearts. It could be a spirit of unforgiveness or jealousy that taunts us to abandon the truth of God in order to follow our selfish desires. Once exploded, any one of these landmines has the ability to paralyze us and stop us from living the life God has given us to live. They rob us of the very faith, hope, love, and joy that He seeks to build into our lives.

Saul had every opportunity to succeed as king. God had anointed and empowered him to rule the nation of Israel. Instead of ruling the people with godly insight, he allowed his heart to be ruled by a spirit of pride. And that very thing led to his downfall.

The enemy is cunning. He knows exactly how to tempt us into disobeying God. He may use the enticement of pride to disarm you, or he could change course and mount an attack with fear, jealousy, sexual sin, or discouragement. There is only one way to combat his wicked efforts, and that is through Jesus Christ. Nothing else will work.

To conquer sin you must admit that you need the Savior. Satan will attempt to use fear, discouragement, thoughts of unforgiveness, pride, and compromise to conquer your heart and emotions. However, God has promised you victory over the very things that the enemy would use for your defeat (Rom. 8:37). You have hope and peace of mind because you are kept by the power of God.

You must settle two things. First, God is greater that any weapon Satan can bring against you. No matter how horrendous Satan's attack may seem, God is all-powerful. Second, to conquer these sins, you must acknowledge that God has forbidden each one. They are landmines that have been laid in your path, but they do not have to lead to your destruction.

You may be tempted to think, *Oh, a little pride never hurt anyone,* but it was a deadly explosion in the life of King Saul, and it is in yours too. Many people mistakenly believe the enemy uses obvious means to draw us off course. However, he rarely takes a predictable route.

Were it not for God's merciful grace and infinite love, any one of us could end up just like King Saul. The wondrous truth that is ours for eternity is that we are not alone. God has not left us without a way through the valleys of life. We have a Savior who is poised to come to our defense the moment we acknowledge our need for His strength and forgiveness.

When you and I fall prey to one of the enemy's devices, the ensuing explosion affects our relationship with God, friends, family members, coworkers, and others. It damages our personal testimony. And if we continue to ignore God's warning, we will get off course, miss His blessings, and experience deep regret.

Over the years, people have asked me how they can learn to discern Satan's wicked schemes. There is a way, but many dismiss it because their hearts are not turned toward God. They want to avoid difficulty and suffering, but they are not willing to commit their lives fully to Jesus Christ.

For them, it is easier to encounter an occasional explosion than to obey God. Their lives lack meaning and true contentment. They are more interested in what the world deems as "right," in style, and important.

Avoiding serious sin is not difficult, especially if you follow the route God has given you to travel. He knows the way through every landmine field. You may be shaking your head and wondering how in the world you could ever hope to stay in tune with God's will, especially when temptation is ready to throw you off the path at every turn.

The truth is, at some point all of us have wondered how we can say no to something that appears so innocent yet contains deadly potential. Oswald Chambers writes,

> If the Spirit of God detects anything in you that is wrong, He does not ask you to put it right [or explain what you have done]; He asks you to accept [God's] light [about your situation], and He will put it right. A child of [God] confesses instantly and stands bared before the Lord; a child of the darkness says—"Oh, I can explain that away."
>
> When once the light breaks and the conviction of wrong comes, be

a child of the light, and confess, and God will deal with what is wrong; if you vindicate yourself, you prove yourself to be a child of the darkness. (*My Utmost for His Highest*)

Victory is realized when we learn to be sensitive to God's Spirit—the Holy Spirit—and to live according to His will and not just our desires. After the Fall, when Adam heard the Lord walking through the garden, he was afraid. He had never felt this emotion before. Then he heard the voice of God asking, "Where are you?" (Gen. 3:9). Adam could deliver only an excuse, "I heard the sound of You in the garden, and I was afraid because I was naked; so I hid myself" (v. 10).

The Lord asked, "Who told you that you were naked? Have you eaten from the tree of which I commanded you not to eat?" (v. 11). For the first time, fear touched Adam's heart, and he responded the way most of us have done when we violate one of God's principles: Adam hid from the Lord.

AVOID TACTICAL ERRORS

Satan believes if he can corner you and pressure you with his vile, sinful suggestion, then there is a chance you may become so discouraged and fearful that you will want to give up. The entire time he is pushing to achieve this goal, he uses extreme tactics of warfare to separate you from God—from the blessings of living in the light of His love and from the love of friends and family.

You do not have to fall victim to Satan's ploys. You can learn to uncover and disarm the enemy's weapons of warfare. When your life is focused only in one direction—toward God—He will guide you safely across the emotional battlefield. He also will show you how to defuse every potential threat.

Therefore, when you feel as though your resolve is about to give way, remember Paul's words to the Corinthians: "No temptation has overtaken you but such as is common to man; and God is faithful, who will not allow you to be tempted beyond what you are able, but with the temptation will provide the way of escape also, so that you will be able to endure it" (1 Cor. 10:13).

God has given you every resource you need to be successful (Josh. 1:7). It all begins with simple faith and love for a holy God who gave His life for you on Calvary's cross. Before His death, Jesus told His followers, "If you continue in My word, then you are truly disciples of Mine; and you will know the truth, and the truth will make you free" (John 8:31–32).

How do you uncover and defuse the landmines that have been laid out in your pathway?

Realize you are in a spiritual war. Many people get up and go out to meet the day without thinking twice about Satan's landmines. Although God never wants us to fear the enemy's threats, we certainly need to be aware of his unyielding desire to rob us of the Lord's blessings. After all, he knows the potential of our lives because we are children of God, and he will do everything within his power to prevent us from enjoying our walk with the Lord. A key step to spiritual victory comes when we acknowledge we have an enemy who poses a real threat. We also need to remember we serve an all-knowing, all-powerful God who loves us with an everlasting love, and He is committed to protecting and providing for us. His love sustains us in times of deep trial and temptation.

We can fight the enemy, but unless we understand the power that has been given to us through Jesus Christ, we will suffer loss. Paul wrote, "The weapons of our warfare are not of the flesh, but divinely powerful for the destruction of fortresses" (2 Cor. 10:4). You must understand the infinite strength that is available to you through Jesus Christ. When you do, you will gain a sense of empowerment that will help you detect the landmines of the enemy.

Once you realize you are accepted, unconditionally loved, and forgiven, you will want to avoid the very things that potentially could bring disaster to you. People who have never learned about God's ways and personal love end up making horrendous mistakes. They become involved in relationships that lead to sin, brokenness, sorrow, and extreme disappointment because they are searching for the very thing that God is offering them with every breath they take.

Many times, people yield to temptation because they are looking for someone who has the ability to meet all their needs. I have counseled young men who have told me, "I believe she can make me happy." This is a common statement and a common mistake. Often people search for the perfect husband or wife, thinking that if they can find that person, all their problems will be solved, but they never are. Problems are a natural part of life, and the only Person who can perfectly meet our needs is Jesus Christ.

As you read through the material in this book, ask Him to open your heart—first, to the love He personally has for you; and second, to those landmines the enemy has strategically placed in front of you. When you become aware of the depth of his deception, you need to turn away from sin and rush into the all-protective, loving arms of Christ, your Lord and Savior.

Trust God and know He will help you. The apostle Peter wrote, "Be of sober spirit, be on the alert. Your adversary, the devil, prowls around like a roaring lion, seeking someone to devour. But resist him, firm in your faith, knowing that the same experiences of suffering are being accomplished by your brethren who are in the world" (1 Peter 5:8–9).

There is knowledge to be gained at every turn with the Lord. We learn to watch for the enemy's crafty deception. And through the presence of the Holy Spirit, we also learn how to stand firm in our faith and not succumb to the enemy's enticements. Adam and Eve were blinded to his sinister plot because they took their eyes off God. Instead of valuing the awesome relationship they had been given, they actually believed that they could gain even more! The reality is that they lost everything—everything but the love of God. His love for them remained steadfast. Out of love for them, He created the garments they wore as they left the garden and went into the rugged landscape of a broken world.

God never abandons us. He did not leave Adam and Eve, and He will never take His love away from you or me. The prophet Jeremiah wrote,

> The LORD's lovingkindnesses indeed never cease,
> For His compassions never fail.
> They are new every morning;
> Great is Your faithfulness. (Lam. 3:22–23)

Perhaps you feel like you have stepped on a horrendous landmine. You have been severely wounded—maimed to the point that you now wonder whether you will ever be emotionally, spiritually, and physically well again. In times when you feel as though you have completely failed, the wondrous love of God always comes shining through the darkness of your situation. When you ask Him to reveal the enemy's landmines that are laid out before you, He will do it. He also will teach you how to disarm the ones that are set and ready to go off so you can walk in the light of His victory and hope each day.

In Ephesians, the apostle Paul told us to

> be strong in the Lord and in the strength of His might. Put on the full armor of God, so that you will be able to stand firm against the schemes of the devil. For our struggle is not against flesh and blood, but against the rulers, against the powers, against the world forces of this darkness, against the spiritual forces of wickedness in the heavenly places. Therefore, take up the full armor of God, so that you will be able to resist in the evil day, and having done everything, to stand firm. (Eph. 6:10–13)

He also admonished us to pray without ceasing, because he knew that the victory God has for us can be won only on our knees (v. 18). If you are struggling, take time to pray. But even more than this, if you want to have the peace that passes all human understanding, ask the Lord to draw you close to Him in prayer. You can do all things through Christ who gives you the strength you need for every problem and situation (Phil. 4:13).

Remember you are not alone. The disciples forgot this one simple truth and detonated a landmine of fear. Out on the open Sea of Galilee with storm clouds gathering, they became fearful. Their eyes were set on their physical surroundings. Instead of recalling the promises of God, they cried out, believing their lives were about to end. So many times we immediately think, *Oh, no! What if this happens? What will I do?* We cave in to fear, but nothing touches our lives unless it has passed through the hands of God—the mighty hands of the omnipotent God, who only has our best interest in mind. It is true that the Holy Spirit had not yet come, and perhaps that was why the disciples struggled. Yet Jesus had told them to go over to the other side of the lake. He had a plan, and it included their safe passage across the Sea of Galilee.

They had seen Jesus stop and pray many times, but they did not follow His example in their time of distress. God wants us to remember that He is with us and will give us the wisdom we need for every situation if we will stop and pray. God has an answer for our every need. But far too often we become paralyzed by our circumstances because we do not call out to the Person who lives inside us.

Nonbelievers have a reason to worry. Their names are not written in the Lamb's Book of Life. Pressures build, problems come, and they do not have the wisdom that God has given to those who have given their hearts and lives to Him.

Storms will come. The winds that blow against your life may feel threatening. However, there is never a moment when you are outside His loving care. You may turn toward sin and even refuse to follow His ways, but He will never stop loving you. He may allow the waves to crest and overflow your boat, but when you cry out to Him, He will save you.

Recall the strength, mercy, and goodness of God. There will be times when you will face serious temptation. It could be something as simple as the urge to lie, gossip, or steal something that you feel is relatively insignificant. Sin, no matter how great it seems or how small it appears, is always important to God because it has the potential to construct a wall between you and the Savior. Do you think Adam and Eve would have accepted Satan's offer if they had fully understood the consequences? And yet we fulfill our urge to sin, though we know the consequences.

When temptation comes, the first thing you need to do is to recall who you are in Christ. As a child of God, you can say no to the enemy's lure. Jesus died on the cross for your sins. His resurrection broke sin's power in your life. Therefore, instead of being controlled and dominated by temptation, you can live free of shame and guilt. We cannot wait until after the landmine explodes to say no to sin. God has given us the Holy Spirit as a guide. He provides the wisdom we need to walk through this life and avoid setting off a landmine.

Even if you yield to sin, you have an Advocate before the Father, who is interceding for you and proclaiming your innocence. John stated, "I am writing these things to you so that you may not sin. And if anyone sins, we have an Advocate with the Father, Jesus Christ the righteous; and He Himself is the propitiation for our sins; and not for ours only, but also for those of the whole world" (1 John 2:1–2).

The English word *advocate* comes from the root word in the Greek meaning "comforter," which is the word used for the Holy Spirit. God is with us at every turn. We are never alone or without the strength and guidance to navigate every situation victoriously (Ps. 18:32). The Comforter, God's Spirit, lives within us, and He has promised to come to our aid, stand beside us in times of trial and difficulty, and be our eternal Counselor.

SOMEONE TO GUIDE YOU ACROSS THE MINEFIELD

I left In Touch Ministries one afternoon a little before two o'clock, and I was sure that I had plenty of time to keep a three o'clock appointment. But as I stopped at a traffic light near the expressway, I caught myself wondering which way I should turn. Traffic in Atlanta is some of the worst in the nation. And I did not want to be late. At that moment, I sensed God's Spirit saying, "Don't go that way—don't get on the expressway." I was not sure that I was hearing Him correctly. Is God really interested in something as minor as traffic on I-85 in Atlanta? The answer is yes! God is concerned about every detail of our lives. And He wants us to know that He is actively involved in all we do. One of the ways we avoid landmines is by heeding His directional guidance. On this day, however, instead of heeding His warning, I headed straight onto the interstate and into traffic! Before I reached the bottom of the entrance ramp, I realized I had made a huge mistake. Traffic was backed up as far as I could see.

Someone reading this may ask, "Does God really speak to us this way?" He does. He speaks to us through His Word, through the Holy Spirit, who lives inside us, and through godly counsel. When your heart is turned toward Him, you will sense His voice directing and guiding you through every situation. This does not mean you will avoid all of life's traffic jams, heartaches, and disappointments, but it certainly does mean He will be with you every step of the way—guiding you, leading you, and answering your prayers.

Once you begin to become aware of God's ways, He will provide the spiritual insight and wisdom to avoid Satan's landmines. The soldier on the battlefield knows there are landmines in front, behind, and along each side, but he cannot become paralyzed with fear. Neither can he forge ahead without considering his adversary's tactics. He has been trained to do a job that requires skill, determination, and foresight. By foresight, I mean the ability to discern the enemy's movement and also the location of the greatest threat.

Wars are not won by rushing into battle without a plan or a map of the combat zone. Likewise, God does not intend for us to go through life blindly—failing to consider the consequences of our actions and the responsibility we have been given as believers. Paul cautioned us to "walk, not as unwise men but as wise, making the most of your time, because the days are evil. So then do not be foolish, but understand what the will of the Lord is" (Eph. 5:15–17).

When you and I step on a landmine, an explosion occurs. We may not immediately know the extent of the damage, but we can predict it will affect our lives in countless ways. This is the reason we need to know how to detect, identify, and protect ourselves from the destruction that comes as a result of the enemy's landmine tactics. God has promised to be our strength in times of difficulty, heartache, and brokenness. The more we learn about Him, the more we will know how to face our enemy and refuse to yield to his battle cries.

TWO

THE LANDMINE OF PRIDE

Years ago while I was on a business trip, I was on an airplane and I found myself talking with a leader of a large Christian organization. We were together for a short period of time, and after a few minutes, he smiled and said, "Charles, we're at the top of our game. No one is doing what we have done. We're the leaders, and I don't think anyone can catch us." Immediately my heart sank. Not because I wanted to be number one, but because I could sense God saying, "Don't ever let that idea cross your mind."

At that moment, it felt as though the Lord had sent an arrow straight into my heart. I knew exactly what He was saying to me. Pride brings destruction, and it does not belong in the life of a believer. At least, not the kind of pride that lifts self up and fails to glorify and honor God. Perhaps this man did not recognize what he had said. Or it may have been that God wanted to send a word of caution to me. Regardless, pride can and does explode God's plan for our lives.

Many times, we begin our Christian walk well. Our focus is set on God, and our hearts are fully committed to Him. Then without warning, pride begins to rise up, preventing us from being all God wants us to be by blinding us to His ways. It tempts us to believe that we know better than He does. If left unchecked, pride will alter our attitude toward God and the route He has chosen for us to take. As believers, we need to be aware of Satan's goal, which is to deeply wound and destroy the lives of God's children. He never gives up on his quest to reach this goal and will wreak as much havoc as possible in the life of a believer.

Of all the struggles discussed in this book, pride is the one that has the most devastating results. Many of our problems result from pride's work in our lives, but too many people fail to realize this. They become prideful over the good things God has given them—jobs, families, children, churches, pastors, education, neighborhoods, and much more.

God is very specific. He hates pride. In fact, it is at the top of His list of sins that He despises: "Pride and arrogance and the evil way / And the perverted mouth, I hate" (Prov. 8:13). The New International Version translates this bluntly: "I hate pride and arrogance, / evil behavior and perverse speech."

Each morning, the enemy lays out his landmines in our lives. If we are not discerning, we will fall prey to his tactics. The landmine of pride can tear a gaping hole in the life of the person who yields to its folly. It is one of Satan's chief modes of operation and favorite weapons of warfare because it tempts us to take our eyes off God and place them on ourselves.

In his book *Power through Prayer,* E. M. Bounds writes, "[Today] somehow, self, not God, rules in the holy of holies. . . . Self-ability in some wicked form has defamed and violated the temple which should be held sacred for God." No matter how hard we try to cover it up, excuse it, or justify it, pride produces the same result—arrogance and rebellion against God.

You may ask, "Isn't it right to have pride in my ability? After all, I have talents and I'm smart. What possibly could be wrong with taking pride in the talents God has given me?" There is nothing wrong with having a sense of pride in doing things well. God gives us talents and abilities to use for His glory, and He wants us to do our best. When we do, we honor Him and His life within us. However, many people fail to honor the Lord with their attitudes. They believe Satan's lies, which tell them they can accomplish whatever they want apart from God. This line of thinking always leads us away from God. And Satan wins the battle.

EXPOSING THE LANDMINE OF PRIDE

God called a young man to the mission field. From the beginning one trial after another assailed him. Each time, according to him, the problem involved key leaders within his organization. Amazingly, he refused to admit that he was part of the problem—it always was someone else. The young man began to tell others that those in authority over him could not do the work as well as he could do it. Soon he became wrapped up in getting credit for his work, but no one would acknowledge what he had done. He was too prideful, and while his friends and coworkers realized this, he did not. A short time later, he became discouraged, disgruntled, and disappointed.

Pride tempts us to believe we are better than someone else. Suddenly this young man felt as though he could no longer work with this organization. Without knowing it, his obedience to God was at stake. He was blinded by his pride and convinced that his only option was to leave the very work God had called him to do. Yet he overlooked one detail: God never rescinds His call. He may change our circumstances or location, but He will never ask us to abandon His will.

The first step this young man took toward defeat came when he did not submit himself to the authority over him. He mistakenly believed that he knew more than the leadership God had placed in his life.

That was Satan's downfall. Because God created him with great beauty and ability, Satan believed he could reign over God and His creation. Once this man decided to follow the deceptive words of his heart, pride had fertile ground in which to grow.

The second step came when he was confronted over his actions and stood steadfast, thinking that he was right and everyone else was wrong. Pride never admits its failures. Instead, the prideful person continues to push forward, blindly seeking self-gratification.

After the first couple of steps, the pathway of pride quickly becomes a slippery slope. Once he convinced himself that he was doing what was best, the young man persisted until he reached a point where he was asked to step down from his post.

He never considered that God uses our circumstances to mold and shape us so we become a reflection of His love to others. He has a work for us to do, and no one can take our place. He may position us in a place of responsibility, which includes some type of difficulty, to accomplish His purpose. At no point are we more important than those around us. We may feel we know more, have more, and can do more than someone else, but the bottom line is that God uses each one of us for His glory. We need to gain the right perspective when signing up to serve Him, and that perspective always includes a humble, contrite heart.

This young man decided not to return to the mission field, though he vowed to continue doing mission work in other arenas. Satan is overjoyed whenever we walk away from the very place God has put us. This is not limited to an office. We can walk away from relationships, responsibilities, and church and community service based on what we mistakenly believe about ourselves.

Pride always overemphasizes self. Our hearts need to be God-focused and not self-focused. What we think, feel, have, want, and desire is not what is important. If you are setting goals without God's input, then you are on pride's trail, and you are heading for trouble.

PRIDE FROM GOD'S PERSPECTIVE

Many times, people are unable to handle the wealth, position, blessing, skill, or talent that God gives them. Uzziah was a perfect example. When he was sixteen, he became king of Judah. The Bible tells us he reigned for fifty-two years in Jerusalem. During that time, "he did right in the sight of the LORD. . . . He continued to seek God in the days of Zechariah, who had understanding through the vision of God; and as long as he sought the LORD, God prospered him" (2 Chron. 26:4–5). Yet a dangerous "however" was built into his life. It was a landmine that lay hidden for years. When the king drew near, it exploded.

Go back to this portion of verse 5, "as long as [the king] sought the LORD, God prospered him." God helped this young man gain many victories. He gave him wisdom so that Judah's army could win the war against the Philistines, who were known for their vicious and tenacious spirit. The armies of the Ammonites and the Arabians were no match for Uzziah and his men, because he followed the Lord. Therefore, the Lord granted him success on and off the battlefield.

He built towers in the wilderness, fortified the city of Jerusalem, and dug many cisterns to water his livestock and irrigate his vineyards. He owned a vast amount of land. The Bible also tells us "the total number of the heads of the households, of valiant warriors [under his command], was 2,600" (2 Chron. 26:12). His elite army numbered more than 307,500 men, "who could wage war with great power, to help the king against the enemy. . . . Hence his fame spread afar, for he was marvelously helped until he was strong" (vv. 13, 15).

Believing all the good things people say about you will lead you to become prideful. Pride always precedes a fall, whereas humility goes a long way toward success. As Uzziah grew in popularity and strength, he began to think that he did not need God. The drift in his devotion to the Lord was subtle—almost undetectable—until one day it broke out in open rebellion. The author of Proverbs has reminded us, "When pride comes, then comes dishonor, / But with the humble is wisdom" (11:2). If we are not careful and discerning, the same attitude that prevailed in Uzziah's life will prevail in our lives too.

When the king realized the strength and ability God had given him, he became proud and no longer relied on the wisdom of the Lord to guide him: "He acted corruptly, and he was unfaithful to the LORD his God, for he entered the temple of the LORD to burn incense on the altar of incense" (2 Chron. 26:16). Offering a sacrifice to God was one of the worst acts Uzziah could have committed. It is the same action that led to King Saul's demise (1 Sam. 13:8–14). In both cases, these men did something that God had anointed the priests to do and no one else. In pride they assumed that no action was beyond their limits.

According to Jewish religious customs, the king was a servant of God and not in a position to intercede before the Lord's throne in this way. All of us have been guilty of jumping ahead of God and doing something that was not ours to do. In this case, the priests were the only ones who could burn incense on the altar. Blinded by his pride, Uzziah stepped out of God's will and did something he was not supposed to do, and the results were disastrous. He surmised that because he was the king, he was above the law and principles of God.

We may not openly refuse to do what God has given us to do, but deep inside this is what is going on when we decide to take a different route or a shortcut around His command to us. We can either obey or dismiss basic principles in His Word. A spirit of pride will always encourage us to turn away from God's way and follow our own line of thinking.

FALLING VICTIM TO PRIDE

In Proverbs 29:23, Solomon wrote, "A man's pride will bring him low, / But a humble spirit will obtain honor." There is an end result to pride—one that we usually want to ignore:

> Pride goes before destruction,
> And a haughty spirit before stumbling.
> It is better to be humble in spirit with the lowly
> Than to divide the spoil with the proud. (Prov. 16:18–19)

Instead of praying and asking God to give us His wisdom for our circumstances, we move forward, believing we know what is best. We may think that we do not need anyone to help us. Perhaps, like King Uzziah, we do not even stop to think. We react with worldly boldness and move forward, never considering what consequences might befall us. Yet we fail to realize that we have stepped onto Satan's landmine and are about to experience serious trouble.

When Uzziah was young, he openly admitted his need for help—especially God's help. He listened to the priests and heeded godly advice. However, when he was older, he began to think he had wisdom and did not need anyone other than himself.

A person falls victim to pride for several reasons:

- self-centeredness
- feelings of inadequacy
- immaturity and an inability to handle responsibility
- inability to handle wealth, position, and the gifts God has given

Pride is an evil, dark snare. It shows no mercy and rarely, if ever, announces its coming. It is sinister and slides into our lives by whispering thoughts of arrogance, conceit, and self-importance. Satan used it in the Garden of Eden, and he uses it today. Then, it was a matter of enticing Adam and Eve to believe they could be like God (Gen. 3:5).

As we read the verses in Genesis recounting the fall of humanity, we find ourselves wanting to shout to Adam and Eve, "Don't do it. Don't take the enemy's bait!" But they did, and we quickly see the results of their failure and pride's emergence in their lives as they cave in to Satan's temptation. Adam and Eve had to leave their home, their place of safety and blessing, because they believed the enemy's lie that told them they could become like God. Instead of rushing to the Lord for help and understanding, they did what King Uzziah did years later. They allowed their hearts' devotion to be swayed by thoughts of prideful temptation.

Azariah the priest entered the temple, saw what Uzziah was about to do, and opposed him, saying, "It is not for you, Uzziah, to burn incense to the LORD, but for the priests, the sons of Aaron who are consecrated to burn incense. Get out of the sanctuary, for you have been unfaithful and will have no honor from the LORD God" (2 Chron. 26:18). Sorrow and sadness are pride's only rewards. Even after hearing this rebuke, the king remained unrepentant and headstrong. "Uzziah, with a censer in his hand for burning incense, was enraged; and while he was enraged with the priests, the leprosy broke out on his forehead before the priests in the house of the LORD, beside the altar of incense" (v. 19).

The priests immediately left Uzziah's presence, and once he realized what he had done, Uzziah fled the house of the Lord, the same thing Adam and Eve did after sinning against God. In their case, however, God had a greater plan in store. He used their failure as an entranceway to proclaim the coming of the Messiah—the One who would overthrow Satan and his evil entrapment of sin and death.

As far as we know, Uzziah never turned back to the Lord in humility. He spent the rest of his life living as a leper in a separate house, cut off from God's presence and His goodness (2 Chron. 26:21). What a sorrowful fate for someone who had such a promising beginning—a man who had spent most of his life living in devotion to God. In the prime of his life, fame became a stumbling block to him. His pride had turned him away from God. This account of King Uzziah's life should be a strong warning to us. Whenever we begin to believe that we are so important that we do not have to be held accountable for what we do or say, then we can be sure we are headed for a fall. Or when we refuse to obey God in a given area, we can expect to experience His discipline in our lives.

The reason is simple: pride isolates us from God. It prevents us from becoming people with hearts devoted solely to Him. This is the reason He hates it. He knows it is a stumbling block, and if left unchecked, it will wreak havoc in our lives. But more than this, pride exalts self and not God. Instead of God receiving the glory for our lives, we seek praise and glory for ourselves.

OVERCOMING PRIDE WITH TRUST

Our sole goal should be to be the best right where God has placed us. We can pray and ask Him to bless us with new challenges, but we need to focus on His plan and timing for our lives. The apostle Peter captured this thought perfectly when he wrote, "Humble yourselves under the mighty hand of God, that He may exalt you at the proper time" (1 Peter 5:6).

There are times when each one of us can sense God drawing near, warning us not to continue along a certain path. For one reason or another, we continue to walk in a direction that is not God's best. Sooner or later, He turns up the pressure to get our attention. Life becomes difficult, and the more we fight against His discipline, the more we will suffer—emotionally, mentally, and physically. Adam and Eve had everything they could hope for, but they wanted more. What they gained at the hands of the enemy were sorrow, separation from the One who loved them unconditionally, and disappointment.

Specific signs tell us we are struggling with pride. While the list is long, it certainly includes the following:

- arrogance
- self-promotion

- lack of giving to God and others

- a selfish attitude

- refusal to listen to the advice of others

- lack of submission to those in authority

- a spirit of rebellion

- bragging

- lack of humble regard for God and others

- the inability to receive a compliment or gift

Pride has many faces. For this reason, God cautions us to be vigilant in our stand against it. If we open a door to it, even a small one, the enemy will take advantage of the opening and rush into our hearts with thoughts that deceive us into thinking much better of ourselves than God desires. He wants you to have a healthy self-esteem, but He also wants you to learn how to handle pride so you will not miss His blessings for you. Here is Satan's trick: he tells us that we must reach certain levels in life to have a sense of worthiness. He also wants us to believe that we do not need anyone else. In other words, we begin to attack life the way he did. To the person who has never accepted Christ as his Savior, the enemy whispers, "You don't need a Savior. Don't bow your knee to anyone. After all, you're the boss of your life."

Believers are not exempt from this type of temptation. It just comes from a different angle: "Don't ask for help. You can do it apart from God. Why tell your friends you are struggling? After all, they will make fun of you and think you are weak." The truth is, each one of us needs the Savior. We need God's wisdom and, most of all, His loving care. We need to know that we are loved just because God is a God of love and He cares for us, no matter what status we hold. Pride often surfaces because a person feels inferior and thinks she needs to be more than what she is.

Don't fall for Satan's tactics. You may think you need to push your way through life, but you don't. Through Jesus Christ you are all you could ever hope to be. Ask God to teach you how to rest in His infinite care. When you learn to do this, you will not only gain a sense of hope, but you will also come to realize how valuable you are in Christ.

THREE

EXPOSING A PRIDEFUL HEART

Of all the sins listed in God's Word, pride is the most destructive. Other sins reflect an unmet need in our lives, but pride is a root for many of our sinful thoughts and actions. Satan mistakenly believes that if he can establish a foothold of pride in our lives, he will have access to our minds, wills, and emotions. When this happens, everything changes. Life begins to revolve around our motives, talents, gifts, and desires.

The truth is that when you are immersed in pride, you rarely consider God at all. Instead, the heart of a prideful person is set on fulfilling his goals and desires. Pride shouts, "I don't need anything or anyone, especially God, because I can make it on my own." No one is self-sufficient. We need each other. We need God first, and then we need one another. God created us this way because He does not want us to work and live independently—separated from His fellowship and the godly fellowship of other believers.

Our world, especially the atmosphere in most corporate businesses, supports, encourages, and promotes a sense of pride. It is not necessarily pride in what we do well. It is pride as a result of who we are and what position we have. You can be proud of doing a good job, but the bottom line is this: all the glory belongs to the Lord. Therefore, it would be better to ask God to give you a godly attitude concerning your job, family, and any other area in which you excel. Yet many people fail to do this. They start out well—believing that if they accomplish certain goals or receive enough awards, they will gain a sense of self-worth. In some cases, pride can actually mask a person's insecurities. One of the most insecure people I have met was an older man who appeared only to want to serve others. After talking with him a few times, I realized that he had a major problem with pride and really only wanted to be noticed for his actions. He may go out to a restaurant and notice that the waiter is not giving him the service he thinks he should receive. His insecurities tell him that he is not worthy of good service, but the side of him that struggles with pride whispers, "How dare he treat you this way? Doesn't he know that you are worthy of his full attention?" A cycle like this one is vicious. On one hand a person feels defeated, but on the other, he also feels that something more is due him. The only way to deal with pride is to admit that there is a problem and a solution is needed.

It doesn't take the enemy long to sense our areas of weakness as we mentioned earlier. He studies our actions and our reactions to life's circumstances. Although he is not omnipotent and could never know us the way Christ knows us, he looks for an opening in our hearts and emotions. Pride is his favorite landmine, because usually we are not particularly interested in detecting its presence. Before long we feel tempted to think, *Look what I have done. I have achieved so much in life.* When our thoughts follow this pattern, we yield to his age-old deception—pride.

While God never stops loving us, He does not dismiss our sinfulness. That day on the airplane, I learned a tremendous lesson concerning the danger of pride. After all, what does it mean to be number one? Does being number one mean that you are bigger or better than someone else? Not necessarily. You may think, *Well, I'm in the business world, and my goal is to be number one.* From the world's perspective, this may seem reasonable.

Pride based on the world's values always breeds competition, which leads to division and strife. Instead of thinking, *I must get ahead [of her or him]*, ask God to help you be the best you can be at work, at home, and in your community. God wants us to learn how to work together to accomplish all that He has given us to do. You may actually end up being number one in some category, and that is great! If you have done your best and yet you come in second or third or even last, then you will gain a sense of satisfaction before God.

Seeking to do your best according to God's ways and principles will bring focus to your life. Before you know it, your heart will begin to reflect His goodness and humility to those around you, and you will know what it truly means to be a godly success. When you honor Him with your life, you will always be a winner, and you won't have to push or shove anyone out of the way to accomplish it.

We also need to consider God's attitude toward pride. He hates it and makes this very clear in His Word. Once we begin to understand His ways, we will know why He feels the way He does. One of the greatest fallouts from pride is that it alienates us from God. Nothing can prevent Him from loving us, but pride can certainly keep us from enjoying His blessings and goodness. This is because pride always lifts itself above others and certainly above God, something He will not abide.

DISCOVERING THE TRUTH ABOUT PRIDE

Even in times when we fail, God's plan for us is at work. Because He knows us completely, He is aware of what it will take to change our prideful hearts. Usually He has to humble us before He can use or bless us. The apostle Peter instructed us to "humble yourselves under the mighty hand of God, that He may exalt you at the proper time" (1 Peter 5:6). Timing is extremely important to God. He knows when we have dealt with pride and when we are ready to receive the goodness He has for us. Far too often, we want to rush ahead of Him. We conveniently forget that before we can be used, we must be broken. We must learn to follow if we want to lead. He is always at work in our lives—molding and shaping us and removing the dross or anything that could prevent us from fulfilling our God-given purpose.

When it comes to pride, King Nebuchadnezzar, like King Uzziah, is a standout. He totally disregarded God's words of warning (Dan. 4). The Lord had spoken to him through a dream telling of his impending downfall. The prophet Daniel interpreted the dream and cautioned him that if he did not "break away" from his sins "by doing righteousness," he would experience a serious humiliation (v. 27). Nevertheless, like many people today, Nebuchadnezzar held fast to his selfishness and egotism.

One day while walking across the rooftop of his palace, he looked out over the city of Babylon and proclaimed, "Is this not Babylon the great, which I myself have built as a royal residence by the might of my power and for the glory of my majesty?" (v. 30). The king had heard God's words of warning through the prophet Daniel, but he ignored them. The Lord had told him that if he did not straighten up, he would become like a beast in the field—grazing on the grass. Two weeks went by and nothing happened. A month came and passed. Then six months went by, and still God had not touched the king's life. He more than likely thought he had gotten away with his prideful attitude and lifestyle. However, after a year, God began to work.

Many times, we yield to sin and think, *Oh, well, that did not matter.* Once a person feels that he has gotten away with sin, he rarely, if ever, thinks, *I won't do that again because I know it displeases God.* Instead, when temptation comes, the prideful person repeats the same action only to a greater degree.

THE CONSEQUENCES OF PRIDE IN THE LIFE OF A BELIEVER

In keeping with His nature, God gave King Nebuchadnezzar the opportunity to repent and turn away from pride. By that time, the king was not interested in pleasing the Lord because his life was totally caught up in pleasing himself. When you look at the world today, does this seem familiar? People sin and then angrily cry out to God, asking why He allowed them to be caught up in such tragic circumstances.

However, not all sorrow and adversity come as a result of disobedience. Some of the disappointments come from living in a fallen world. Many come because we have ignored God. Like the young man mentioned earlier who left the mission field, we simply leave our post without being given the command to do so. Or thinking that we know what is needed, we fail to obey God's commands. This is the fact of pride, and it is not something that God will allow us to have in our lives.

King Nebuchadnezzar became more prideful with each day until his heart had grown cold to the things of God. After a year, God did exactly what He said He would do. He allowed the king to suffer a great emotional, mental, and physical fall, and he ended up eating grass like the wild beasts of the field.

Pride hinders our fellowship with God. God tells us in His Word that we cannot serve two masters. We cannot be loyal to Him and be self-centered and self-serving. Only one Person is worthy of all our praise, and that is Jesus Christ. If you are more interested in living life your way than you are in pleasing God, then you are dealing with pride, and God will have to remove it.

Pride leads to broken relationships with others. It prevents us from loving and caring about those around us. Instead of thinking about what they can do to help and serve others, prideful individuals think only about how they can benefit from a relationship. It is hard to be around someone who constantly seeks to be the center of attention. If you are serious about removing pride from your life, ask God to show you how you can serve someone else. Turn the thought of praise away from yourself, and place it on the Lord or even someone else who has been supportive and encouraging.

The truth is, from God's perspective, no one is greater than someone else. We are all standing on equal ground. No one is going to be a standout in heaven. God loves each one of us equally, and He wants us to love one another with the same type of love. He saved us from sin, and He is the source of our worth. Take Him out of our lives, and we have nothing of eternal value to offer. If you think you have done something to create a name or position for yourself, then you may want to reconsider your evaluation because God is the only reason we have life. The opportunity to live it abundantly is a gift of grace from Him.

Pride blocks God's blessings and often causes us to lose our rewards. Imagine all the goodness that God has stored up for you! It is more than you can comprehend. Most people tap into just a small portion of the spiritual wealth that is theirs because they are so busy working, striving, reaching, and longing for something more materially. God tells us, "Seek first His kingdom and His righteousness, and all these things will be added to you" (Matt. 6:33).

If you choose to follow your own path in your own strength, you will miss the blessings that God has for you to enjoy. You may think, *But I must reach this goal. I need to be the chairperson or the vice president. If not, I'm a failure.* The truth is, if you do not tap into God's will for your life, all the success this world has to offer will not come close to the success that God has for you.

God's blessings offer a sense of fulfillment and peace that you will never be able to achieve on your own. His call to you is to be faithful in what you have been given to do. I believe there will be many people who are heartbroken in heaven because they will look at what they have accomplished and see the true value of what they spent a lifetime achieving. It will be wood, hay, and stubble next to the blessings God had for them.

Pride lessens the fullness of relationship with Him. Pride darkens our hearts to the light of God's truth and keeps us from experiencing the joy and hope that come from living fully free in Him. Pride binds our hearts to thoughts of worldly ambitions and desires. Instead, we can become tethered to Satan's lies and his earthbound limitations, especially if we buy into the fact that we have to have more of everything to be happy.

However, when we joyfully give up our rights to a life we choose in order to know Christ and to make Him known to others, the tendency to be prideful diminishes. This is the bottom line to experiencing true contentment and fulfillment. As long as we are worried about who is getting ahead and who has more or as much as we do, we will never be at a point where we can truly rest in God's care. The Lord may give us many blessings, but unless we are fully surrendered to Him, the corner office, the new home or car, or the perfect relationship will not satisfy us. Like Adam and Eve, we will always want more and always receive less.

Pride decreases our effectiveness as a leader. Whether you are a leader of a few people, a leader in your church, Sunday school, or a large organization, pride prevents you from being an effective leader. People want to follow someone they trust—someone who has their best interest in mind. However, prideful leaders are focused on what they can gain. There is what I call "static" in their minds and hearts. They fail to see objectives clearly because they are wrapped up in their dreams, goals, and desires. I have seen this in the business world. I've also seen it at work in ministries. A leader is hired, she begins with a humble spirit, and then others give her a considerable amount of recognition. Instead of thanking God for the success, the leader steps back and thinks, *They are right. Look what I have done. I'm important.*

God hates pride because it shifts the glory from Him to us, and we are not the ones who need to be honored. Is it right for us to say "thank you" for the awards and compliments we receive? Absolutely! He has created us to be successful, and He is training us to reign one day with Him. However, if the focus of our hearts is set on our dreams, goals, achievements, and desires, then we will not be interested in following His will or plan for our lives. We will want to live our way, and then what we will receive in return will be very disappointing. Therefore, ask Him to give you a humble, grateful heart. Look for opportunities to praise and honor Him for the goodness and mercy He has extended to you.

Legendary Olympic runner Eric Liddell did this very thing. He ran with pure abandonment, never hesitating to give God the glory. "The Lord guides me," he told one reporter. As word of his Christian faith spread through England, many wondered whether he would display the same zeal on the track. Liddell silenced skeptics in the AAA Championships in London in July 1923 when he won the 220-yard dash and the 100-yard dash. The next year, in the 1924 Paris Olympics, he won a gold medal for the 400-meter race. "When I run," he said unashamedly, "I feel God's good pleasure."

Are you running life's race according to your rules and the world's desires? If you are, then you will feel the enormous weight of others' expectations and demands. If you are running according to God's game plan, then you will sense His good pleasure lifting you and giving you the strength to win the race.

Pride entices us to favor people who build up our egos. Everyone wants to feel accepted and loved. The best way to rid your life of pride is to surround yourself with people who care for you for the right reasons and not just to stroke your ego. Pride is a stumbling block for many leaders because there is a tendency to be surrounded by those who say what they believe the leader wants to hear.

If you find that this is true of you, then you need to ask your friends to be honest with you. The 360-review process may have originated in the workplace as a way for employers to learn more about their abilities and habits, but the concept is gaining ground in the home where family members review one another and give honest answers that foster accountability. On a lesser scale, we can do this for one another by encouraging our friends and family members to provide honest, healthy feedback on our character and the roles we play in their lives. Are we the type of friend they can call on in times of trouble, or would they say that we think more about ourselves than about helping in times of crisis and trouble? Are we givers or just receivers? Do we have an eternal perspective, or do we like to think only about how our problems affect us? If we hear them use words such as *pride* and *selfishness,* then we know that we have triggered a landmine within our lives that could prevent us from enjoying the fellowship of others. More important, we will never be able to experience the fullness of God's love and acceptance until we abandon our need to be first and to be recognized above others. Jesus was a servant, and following in His footsteps should be our greatest desire.

When you step on a landmine, it will explode, and usually it will do horrendous damage. Pride is a landmine that cannot be ignored because it is linked to a series of other landmines, including jealousy, envy, laziness, fear, compromise, unforgiveness, and more.

Pride sets the stage for us to make foolish mistakes. The enemy is waiting for the right opportunity to tempt us to venture away from God's principles with words of pride and self-reliance. The prideful person will cease to seek godly wisdom and advice. He will think that he is too smart to need someone else's help or insight; that he can handle everything alone; that he needs to be the one who does the project, completes the tasks, or achieves the goal because no one else can do it as well. Remember, pride isolates. Satan wants you to be on your own doing what you think only you can do. He knows when you make a mistake and your world begins to crash around you, you will not have a godly support system to help sustain you. You will be alone in your pride, and you will experience the painfulness that comes from this loneliness.

Pride shuts down the work of the Holy Spirit in our lives. When we become prideful, God's discernment within our lives fades. We begin to make horrendous decisions because we no longer have His wisdom available. It is as if we are spoiled children demanding our way until finally our mother or father tells us, "Fine. Do it your way." When we do, we usually end up making foolish decisions and reaping the consequences.

Discerning people know the difference between right and wrong. They can sense God saying, "Stop!" "Wait!" or "Slow down!" But the prideful person never gives an ear to God's instruction and runs headlong into trouble. If this characterizes your life, you can change your direction right now by praying and asking God to forgive you and to help you overcome the pride that is preventing you from being the man or woman He has designed you to be. Don't think for a minute that after eating a few mouthfuls of grass that King Nebuchadnezzar would fail to warn you. He would shout, "All the pride and position this world has to offer is not worth spending one day outside the goodness and presence of God."

Pride breeds prayerlessness. The prideful person does not want to connect with God—through worship or prayer. She may attend church for appearance's sake, but actual devotion is missing. Prayer keeps us in line with God's will. In His presence there is fullness of joy. It is also the one place we can sense His unconditional love toward us. It is the only channel by which you and I can communicate with Him. It also is the channel through which He reaffirms His ways to us. If we do not understand His ways, we miss so much. Knowing God and allowing Him to live through us opens us to receive His blessings in ways we cannot imagine. It is only through prayer that we grow to know Him and love Him better each day.

Pride causes us to emphasize self more than God. We begin to view ourselves as being important. We hear comments like, "You are fantastic!" and we begin to think that we are. A little popularity, a few compliments, and we forget who has given us the ability to achieve our goals, be successful, or see our dreams become a reality. Often when this happens, God will step into our lives and, if necessary, place us on "the shelf" for a season. He is not going to honor our work when pride is involved. We also need to remember that Satan is never complacent. He doesn't brush his hands together and walk away, thinking that he has done enough for now. He is relentless in his approach and will continue to pursue us with the goal of destroying our witness and testimony for the Lord. Until the day the Lord returns or God calls us home to be with Him, we must remain vigilant in our spiritual walk with Him.

The evidences of pride in one's life are obvious:

- the desire to be number one or first
- continual reference to oneself
- the longing to be the center of attention
- a need to seek the praise and compliments of others
- a desire to dress in such a way as to gain the attention of others
- a need to be seen in prominent places
- unwillingness to help people who are less fortunate
- a rebellious spirit
- a tendency to take credit for something that someone else did
- refusal to do menial tasks

- refusal to apologize when wrong
- an attitude of self-sufficiency

THE CONSEQUENCES OF PRIDE

Pride prevents us from experiencing a personal, intimate relationship with the Savior. Jesus tells us in His Word that there is only one way to the Father and that is through Him. He commands us to be humble before Him. Pride, however, encourages us to exalt ourselves. Peter wrote, "Clothe yourselves with humility toward one another, for God is opposed to the proud, but gives grace to the humble. Therefore humble yourselves under the mighty hand of God, that He may exalt you at the proper time" (1 Peter 5:5–6). Pride literally erects an emotional wall between the Savior and us.

If you want to know God, you must come to a point where you accept His Son—the Lord Jesus Christ. This means surrendering your life to the One who loves you perfectly and without regret. He gave His life for you on the cross so that you could have an eternal relationship with the heavenly Father.

Nicodemus was a Pharisee and a member of the Sanhedrin. He was a scholar and a teacher who hungered to know God. After hearing Jesus speak on several occasions, he found the Savior alone one evening. In the quiet of the night, he looked at Jesus with searching eyes and said, "Rabbi, we know that You have come from God as a teacher; for no one can do these signs that You do unless God is with him. . . . How can a man be born when he is old? . . . How can these things be?" (John 3:2, 4, 9). I believe that intuitively Nicodemus knew Jesus had much more to offer than anything he had learned in all the books and scrolls he had read up to that point. "For God so loved the world," Christ told him, "that He gave His only begotten Son, that whoever believes in Him shall not perish, but have eternal life" (John 3:16).

Nicodemus lived to see these words become a reality in his own life. Jesus died for his sins and ours too. Through faith in God's Son, we gain eternal life and an opportunity to have a personal relationship with God. There is no other way to the Father except through faith in Jesus. All the knowledge this world has to offer cannot save you from an eternal death. There is only one way, one God, one destiny. Those who come to Jesus Christ through faith will not perish but will have eternal life (John 6:47; 10:27–30).

SEVEN STEPS TO SUCCESSFULLY DEALING WITH PRIDE

The first thing you can do to combat pride is to realize that pride is present in your life. Before you can deal with pride, you must acknowledge it. You do not have to continue living in a state of pride. You need to confess that you have a problem in this area. Before God can fully change your heart, you must make a decision to turn away from the very sin that is separating you from Him. He sees your desire to repent and draws closer as you draw close to Him and seek His restoration and forgiveness. However, many people find this very hard to do. Pride has so captured their hearts that they refuse to admit there is a problem.

Second, ask God to forgive you for being prideful. Tell Him that you do not want anything in your life that would separate you from Him or prevent you from experiencing His best.

Third, pray that He will give you the ability to turn away from pride. It is one thing to confess pride, but you cannot stop here. Go all the way and ask Him for the strength to lay aside any pride that you may have in your life. Realize that there will be times that God removes pride by allowing you to face disappointment and even times of brokenness. Remember, though, that He breaks us only in order to bless us. Brokenness is always a pathway to blessing.

Fourth, pray that He will set a hedge of protection around your life. Also, ask Him to give you the discernment to detect the landmine of pride before you approach it. One of the best ways to defuse conceit and arrogance is to serve somebody else—not to receive credit—but to learn humility and the goodness that comes from being submitted to the Lord fully and completely. God rewards obedience, and His greatest desire is for you to obey Him so you can experience all that He has planned for you.

Fifth, remember where you came from and how far God has brought you. Over time, many believers forget the foundation of their salvation. The phrase "such were some of you" is forgotten. They overlook the fact that they once yielded to sin and that they are doing so even now through judging others. In 1 Corinthians 6:11, the apostle Paul wrote, "You were washed . . . you were sanctified . . . you were justified in the name of the Lord Jesus Christ and in the Spirit of our God." He admonished us never to forget that Christ died for us—for our sins. Pride beckons us to look down on those who are trapped in sin. Yet God calls us to pray even harder for those who have drifted in their devotion or never made a commitment to Christ.

You do not have to dwell on the past, but you certainly need to remember that each day God's grace preserves your life. The moment you allow ingratitude to grow within your heart, you are on the verge of stepping on the landmine of pride. Avoid it; keep your heart turned toward God, and He will fill it with joy that exceeds anything you can imagine.

Sixth, ask God to help you recall the good things that He has done in your life, and stop comparing yourself to someone else. He created you in love, and He has a plan that only you can fulfill. No one else is exactly like you. You are precious in His sight, and He loves you more than anyone possibly can or ever will. When you draw comparisons between yourself and another believer, you open a door for pride to enter. Remember what we said earlier: we are all on the same level, going in the same direction. Coveting what others have—whether it is a personality trait, a life position, or a material possession—is dangerous. Once again, this activity changes the way we view life. It alters our hearts because it fosters pride and erases any gratitude we may have toward God for the good things He has given. Therefore, be faithful right where you are— praise Him for what you have been given, keep your eyes set on Him, and do your best.

Seventh, be willing to experience adversity. None of us would raise our hands and volunteer to experience disappointment or sorrow. However, God does His greatest work in the hard times. This is when we need to remember that whatever drives us to God is always good for us. Nothing does this more effectively than trouble, heartache, and adversity, which are mighty tools in God's hands. If life is running really well, we may not think seriously about how God views us. But if we are confronted with a deep disappointment or a resounding sorrow, we will respond by crying out to Him. When we do, a wondrous thing happens: He turns in our direction—opens His arms and draws us close.

The landmine of pride is one of the most deadly weapons in Satan's arsenal. It is the very landmine that caused Satan's fall from heaven, and it can certainly wreak havoc in your life. You won't lose your salvation, but you will experience a loss by allowing your life to become prideful. Once you understand that God loves you deeply, you will want to turn away from the very pride that separates you from Him. The best way to avoid pride and the other landmines that Satan has placed along your path is to surrender your life to Christ. As long as pride holds a prominent place in your heart, Christ is not Lord. Even if you have accepted Him as your Savior, you must choose to turn every area over to Him and allow Him to live His life through you. When you do, He will bless you in ways you never thought possible.

FOUR

THE LANDMINES OF JEALOUSY AND ENVY

As a youth, Joseph probably was carefree and did not stop to think about what he was saying or even doing. At times, words may have fallen out of his mouth without restraint—they were full of life and what he believed would come true. His brothers usually cringed and held back from making any obvious comment that would reveal their slow-burning anger and jealousy against him.

He was Rachel's son. Though Jacob had other wives, Rachel was the one he loved, and that made him favor Joseph (Gen. 29:18; 37:3). He made this very clear through his actions, which probably fed Joseph's youthful arrogance. The Bible tells us that "Joseph brought back a bad report about [his brothers] to their father" (Gen. 37:2). It goes on to say, "[Jacob] loved Joseph more than all his sons, because he was the son of his old age; and he made him a varicolored tunic [or a coat of many colors]" (Gen. 37:3).

Without knowing it, Jacob, whom God later renamed Israel, had set the stage for one of the most aggressive struggles a person can face: jealousy and envy. If not addressed and resolved, these have the potential to cause deep strife within our lives. And if they are not defused, they can eat a hole in a person's heart and emotions. We may become jealous of others because we think they have more than we do. Such was the case with Joseph's brothers (Gen. 37:11). They felt left out, overlooked, and unappreciated by their father. Joseph, on the other hand, had been given whatever his heart desired. And he also had just received a multicolored coat, which represented his father's love and favor.

EXPOSING THE TRUTH ABOUT JEALOUSY

Jealousy is a landmine that strikes hard. It has the ability to cause a great deal of harm to our faith, preventing us from enjoying God's richest blessings. Just because we see someone advancing before us does not mean that God is withholding His goodness toward us. He may be simply preparing us for what will come in the future. He wants to bless us, but He also wants to reveal the deeper motivation of our hearts. That was what happened in the lives of Joseph's brothers. The first time they witnessed their father's love for him, they might have cringed. The second time, they might have rolled their eyes in disgust. The third time, they were ready to strike out in frustration and anger. From that point on, jealousy began to build.

Whenever you sense feelings of envy and jealousy growing, you must answer two questions: *How will I respond to the jealous feelings, and how will I deal with my actions, which usually include feelings of anger?* Before launching a full-blown assault on the person you believe is your offender, you need to remember Satan's primary goal: shift your focus away from God and onto your circumstances. He wants you to become jealous, distracted, and prideful.

Satan loves for your eyes to become fixed on yourself—your feelings, your rights, and your needs. He will push against your thoughts with words such as, "What about me? I deserve more out of life—a new home, a new car, new friends, and a larger bank account." The enemy will stop at nothing to create an atmosphere brimming with jealousy, which can lead to other problems such as discouragement and anger. Joseph's brothers were sure their father was overlooking them. They mistakenly assumed their lack of importance. Therefore, thoughts of jealousy burned deep within their hearts until they acted on their emotions and did something that caused great pain within their own lives and their father's for many years.

You and I do not have to yield to the enemy's temptation. We can learn to overcome feelings of jealousy and gain a true understanding of our worth in God's eyes. Maybe we are not appreciated by some of the people we know and work beside each day. However, He has chosen us. He loves with an everlasting love, and He has a plan for our lives. This plan, however, may not unfold at the same time as God's plan for another person. We need to be patient and wait for God to give us His blessings at the right time. It can be tempting to wonder, *Lord, what about me?* Often people become jealous without knowing that God has something good headed their way. When we become jealous, we risk missing His best gifts because we are focused only on what we do not have. When we choose this route, a lot of time can be wasted entertaining feelings of heartache, frustration, worry, and envy.

Don't become caught in this trap. God knows your future. He also knows what it will take to prepare you for the blessings that He has for you. There may be times when you are just not ready to receive His goodness. At these times He allows you to face situations in which you have to battle thoughts of jealousy. The process could take weeks, months, or even years. The truth is that before you can deal with jealousy appropriately, you must come to the conclusion that God loves you and He has not forgotten you. You may feel forgotten in a relationship, on your job, or even in your church, but He will never overlook you.

DETONATING THE LANDMINE OF JEALOUSY

When you set the focus of your heart on pleasing God, you may go through times of envy when you feel as though your Christian walk is leading you nowhere fast. However, as long as you maintain your desire to live for Him, He will show you how to right your course so that you do not drift away from the center of His love. Remember, God's number one goal is to draw you into a close relationship with His Son. Feelings of jealousy can blind you to His goodness. It is like seeing a glass half empty instead of seeing it half full. If you only see your life in light of what you don't have when compared to someone else, you will never learn to enjoy what God has given you. Becoming hooked by feelings of jealousy means you are out of step with God's plan. While He has the ability to deal with the smaller matters in your life, He never loses sight of His larger plan, which is to draw you into an intimate relationship with Him. Jealousy does not belong in the life of a believer because it goes against the very heartbeat of God.

You may be thinking, *Doesn't God say He is jealous for us?* The answer is yes, but it is a different type of jealousy; it is *not* the kind of jealousy that leads to envy and sin. It is a protective jealousy that is much greater than a loving parent would have for a son or daughter. God is not envious *of* us; He is jealous *for* us, which means He desires our fellowship and love. He has a passionate commitment for us because we rightfully belong to Him and He wants to protect us from evil. Therefore, He watches over us with extreme care.

In Joshua 24, we read, "Joshua said to the people, 'You will not be able to serve the LORD, for He is a holy God. He is a jealous God; He will not forgive your transgression or your sins. If you forsake the LORD and serve foreign gods, then He will turn and do you harm and consume you after He has done good to you'" (vv. 19–20). Joshua's words sounded a strong warning to the nation of Israel not to allow anything in their lives that would hamper their fellowship with Him. Over the course of time, Israel's devotion to God waned. They began to observe the devotion of their enemies to false gods and wanted to follow this pattern of pagan worship. It seems impossible to believe, but even after all that God had done for the nation of Israel, they began to incorporate pagan worship into their lives, much to God's displeasure.

Far too often, we do the same thing by devoting time and energy to the gods of this age—material wealth, social position, and much more. If we do not receive what we think we should, we become jealous, and in doing so we overlook God's goodness and holiness. We sidestep His love and miss a wonderful opportunity for a deeper relationship with Him. We end up worshiping the gods of this age and wonder why our lives are so empty, incomplete, and unsatisfying. This is what jealousy tempts us to do—think more of the things we do not have than of the blessings that God has given.

Israel did not obey God and ended up following after other gods. They may have continued in their worship of the Lord, but their lives were influenced by the pagan nations they were sent to conquer. Learning to live apart from jealousy may seem hard to do, but it is not. To accomplish this we must come to a point where we realize that partial obedience is not obedience. In other words, you cannot be kind to a person in her presence and then behind her back spew out words of jealousy and envy against her.

Learning to let go of jealous feelings is a process. At some point, everyone has been tempted to envy what another person has. But if we could see what God sees, we would never struggle with this feeling. He tells us it is wrong because He knows it divides our minds and creates an atmosphere of resentment in our hearts. As with all sin, He wants us to acknowledge it to Him and then turn away from it. Israel did not do this. They embraced foreign gods so their devotion to God was divided and they quickly drifted away from Him.

Whenever we allow the enemy to divert our focus from God through jealousy or another landmine, we will experience a certain degree of spiritual defeat. In a very real way, the various landmines mentioned in this book are connected. Often one explosion can lead to another.

Jealousy can create an atmosphere of anxiety and fear within our hearts. The old adage "one thing leads to another" is very true. It also describes the tactical outline that Satan has in mind. He believes he has set up the battlefield to his advantage. If we have a problem with jealousy, we need to know that this is not the only landmine that we will trigger. The flow will go something like this: jealousy leads to envy and envy to anger and anger to fear. The cycle will continue until we become paralyzed or until we turn to God and ask for His intervention.

Anyone who trusts God for the future should never be threatened by the blessings given to another person. If Joseph's brothers had acted with maturity, the outcome could have been much different. However, we also have to account for God's providential involvement in the situation. Though Jacob's sons responded in envy and hatred, God used their sin to change the course of a nation.

If you are struggling with jealousy, you are probably experiencing problems in other areas. You may have forgotten that "the LORD God is a sun and shield; / The LORD gives grace and glory; / No good thing does He withhold from those who walk uprightly" (Ps. 84:11). You also may have overlooked the fact that God has a plan for your life. He has not forgotten you. Coveting what another person has only prevents you from enjoying the journey that He has mapped out. Ask Him to forgive you for any envy that you have toward another. Be honest. Is there someone you do not like being around because you feel threatened by what God has given him? God is only interested in one thing, and that is how you live your life before Him. Make sure you are in step with Him and you will have much more than you can imagine.

JEALOUSY IS A MATTER OF CHOICE

Let me say one thing about temptation: the enemy uses it to draw us into his web of deception. The key to overcoming sin is to realize the great sense of worth we have in God's eyes. Sin pulls us down and takes an edge off who we are in Christ. We may think no one will ever know what we have done, but God does and He is the One who counts the most. As stated earlier, sin always involves choice. When we are jealous, we have made a choice to be envious of others. Over the years, there have been some tremendously difficult moments in my life. However, every time I set my heart on pleasing Him, He always provides the answer I need. What are you facing today that only He can solve? You may be thinking, *What does all of this have to do with the landmine of jealousy?* Everything—learning to obey God starts with a heart that is turned toward Him. Anything that threatens to erode our relationship with God should be avoided at all costs.

Joseph's brothers never considered God's will and purpose for their futures. They saw how Joseph was being treated, and they felt left out, threatened, jealous, and angry. Sin always begins with a single thought. It is at this point where we can choose to hold on to it or let it pass through our minds. If we cling to it, we will end up doing what Joseph's brothers did. We will take matters into our own hands and become jealous along the way.

After having a dream where he saw a vision of the future, Joseph didn't waste a moment in delivering its message to his brothers. The dream God gave him revealed that one day his brothers would bow down and serve him. He told them: "We were binding sheaves in the field, and lo, my sheaf rose up and also stood erect; and behold, your sheaves gathered around and bowed down to my sheaf" (Gen. 37:7).

We can easily imagine the outrage his brothers felt, and certainly that was their reaction: "Are you actually going to reign over us? Or are you really going to rule over us?" (v. 8). They were furious! Then Joseph added fuel to an already explosive situation by emphasizing what he believed the future would hold: one day he would rule over his brothers. If we had been at Joseph's side, we may have advised him to wait and not reveal what he had seen in his dream. More than likely, a hint of pride tempted him to flaunt what God was going to do. Plus,

Scripture tells us that he truly was Jacob's favorite, something he dangled in front of his brothers.

Jealousy quickly came to the surface in their lives. Then, when they were alone and away from their father, they acted on their envious desires. They removed the coat that Joseph's father had given him. In their rage, they threw Joseph into the pit and left him. However, a little later feelings of guilt began to consume their hearts. His brothers retrieved him from the pit, but they turned around and sold him to a band of traveling merchants.

While Joseph survived his brothers' jealousy, he spent years in bondage. Once the merchants reached Egypt, they sold him as a slave. When we think about it, everyone involved in this story was bound by sorrow or shame. Jealousy creates this kind of atmosphere, but we do not have to live life under this sort of shadow. When we come to a point where we understand how important we are to God, feelings of jealousy will fade. After all, why would we want any more than what God, in His goodness and grace, has given to us right now? What could be more important, more rewarding, than living the life He has called us to live?

WINNING THE STRUGGLE OF JEALOUSY

Many of the years Joseph spent in captivity were far from enjoyable. He was jailed and feared that he would never see his father again. One thoughtless act of jealousy had changed the entire course of his life. Yet he was not alone. God was with him. Therefore, he had a sense of deep peace within his heart (Gen. 39:21). Though his circumstances did not change immediately, he remained steady in his trust in God.

His brothers did not fare as well. They retrieved their brother's tunic from the pit where they had placed him, soaked it in animal's blood, and carried it to their father along with a story of how Joseph had been killed by a wild beast (Gen. 37:31–33). They wanted to avoid punishment at all costs. Feelings and thoughts of jealousy led to only one destination—

sin. Not only did Joseph's brothers plot to kill him, but they acted on their feelings, and they had to lie to cover up what they had done.

In reality, they did not know what happened to Joseph. This only made their guilt grow greater. They could not tell their father what they had done, nor could they admit the way they felt. Throughout the years, the memory of their actions never faded. Doctors now believe that so much of the sickness and even depression and anxiety people experience comes as a result of feeling jealous, guilty, angry, hostile, and unforgiving toward others. We may hear people boast that they are not bothered by their feelings of anger or some other strong negative emotion, but they are. It is common knowledge that landmines such as unforgiveness, fear, jealousy, envy, and more take a toll on us physically. We must work through these emotional landmines or face the consequences, which usually show up in our physical health.

If left unaddressed, jealousy and envy will become evident. We may end up losing sleep, isolating ourselves from others, or becoming critical toward a person or an organization. We also may develop an unforgiving spirit that leads to bitterness. God wants us to live in harmony with others. He never planned for us to become envious of what those around us have or what they do. His plan for our lives is one of peace, hope, and steadfast faith, especially in times of difficulty. Life may change, but God's hope within us never does. If our faith is fixed on Him, then when the temptation to trip a landmine comes, we will recall our accountability for our lives before Him. There would be no room for jealousy if we would remember who holds our lives within His righteous hand.

Most people probably would find it hard to admit that they struggle with jealousy. Few, if any, would readily admit they are envious of a friend who has just accepted a proposal to get married or a promotion at work. It is easy to say, "I want people to enjoy all that God has for them." It is another thing to actually live with this intent. Without fail, many people notice the family who has enough money to purchase a new home along with a new car. We openly ask, "How do they do it?" with a hint of jealousy in our voices. Friends come to you excited about a trip they are about to take. Instead of rejoicing with them, your emotions tighten, and you think about how it seems that you never get ahead or receive a break.

Many times, the circumstances will not make sense from our perspective. However, from God's vantage point, they make perfect sense. He used Joseph's plight to prepare him for a very great service, and each one of us is being prepared for a great service. But God always brings hope to our hopeless situations. Ultimately He used Joseph's captivity to save an entire nation from annihilation.

Even the apostle Peter had to be reminded of this very thing. After the Resurrection, he asked Jesus about the apostle John. "Peter, turning around, saw the disciple whom Jesus loved following them; the one who also had leaned back on His bosom at the supper and said, 'Lord, who is the one who betrays You?' So Peter seeing him said to Jesus, 'Lord, and what about this man?' Jesus said to him, 'If I want him to remain until I come, what is that to you? You follow Me!'" (John 21:20–22).

This is a perfect answer to the struggle of jealousy—"What is that to you? You follow Me!" In other words, focus your heart on the Savior. Quit keeping score and tallying up nonexistent points. When your eyes are set on Jesus, you will not be concerned about who is getting ahead or who is lagging behind. James wrote,

> Who among you is wise and understanding? Let him show by his good behavior his deeds in the gentleness of wisdom. But if you have bitter jealousy and selfish ambition in your heart, do not be arrogant and so lie against the truth. This wisdom is not that which comes down from above, but is earthly, natural, demonic. For where jealousy and selfish ambition exist, there is disorder and every evil thing. But the wisdom from above is first pure, then peaceable, gentle, reasonable, full of mercy and good fruits, unwavering, without hypocrisy. And the seed

whose fruit is righteousness is sown in peace by those who make peace. (James 3:13–18)

This passage reminds us that we will face the normal temptation of jealousy. It is a part of life that we must turn away from in order to experience the grace and peace that God wants us to enjoy. However, many people find this hard to do. A jealous thought passes through their minds, and they are hooked by it. James told us when we live our lives for Jesus Christ, we will be focused not on what we do not have but on what He has given us through the life of His Son.

Many believers fight vicious battles with pride and jealousy because they have never fully submitted their hearts to the lordship of Jesus Christ. They hold on to negative, defeating thoughts because they believe if they let go, they will not get what they want. They are rushing through each day with the hope of getting ahead when actually they are falling behind. Whatever is earthly, natural, fleshly, carnal, and demonic does not fit who we are as followers of Jesus Christ.

"The deeds of the flesh," wrote Paul, "are evident . . . immorality, impurity, sensuality, idolatry, sorcery, enmities, strife, jealousy, outbursts of anger, disputes, dissensions, factions, envying, drunkenness, carousing, and things like these, of which I forewarn you, just as I have forewarned you, that those who practice such things will not inherit the kingdom of God" (Gal. 5:19–21). In other words, if we continue to practice these sins, our actions are evidence of our lack of love for and devotion to Christ.

In contrast, the fruit of the Spirit includes love, joy, peace, patience, kindness, goodness, faithfulness, gentleness, and self-control (Gal. 5:22–23). Jealousy and envy are listed as sins that are carnal, fleshly, and demonic. We are sons and daughters of the living God. The next time we decide to envy another's position, wealth, or achievement, we need to consider the source of the temptation and the architect of this destructive landmine.

Often when we are tempted to become jealous, we are afraid that someone will take our place. There is a possessiveness hidden within jealousy that is very dangerous.

Jesus instantly knew this and confronted Peter when he raised a question about John's future (John 21:21–22). God was planning to use both men mightily. There was no need for competition.

Envy comes when we see someone gain a certain position that we believe we should hold. We can become so caught up in what another person has that we lose sight of what God has given us. Often when this happens, God will reset our thinking by allowing us to experience difficulty or trial. While He does not cause the adversity, He certainly uses it to get our attention and draw us back to Himself.

The next time you are tempted to dismiss the power of jealousy and envy by thinking, *No one is perfect; everyone has a little sin in his life*, you need to consider the consequences of your thoughts and actions. The truth is, everyone wants to be accepted, loved, and blessed. But when you allow jealousy to set up shop in your life, you end up feeling rushed, angry, and very critical of yourself and others.

A VICTIM OF JEALOUSY

Like Joseph, you may be a victim of jealousy. Someone is envious of you, and you can feel the heat of anger and resentment toward you. Most people are hesitant to admit they have a problem in this area. They will slough the suggestion off, convincing themselves that they really do not feel jealous or they did not mean for us to take their critical words the way we did. All the while, a raging fire is burning deep within them.

Or perhaps you have longed to reach a certain goal and have come up short several times. It seems that friends are recognized before you and applauded for their efforts while you are standing on the sidelines wondering whether God will ever give you a chance to demonstrate your talent or potential.

Time is a key factor in God's battle plan. Though Joseph's brothers treated him poorly, God did not rush to his aid. Instead, He preserved Joseph's life. He was with him in his time of sorrow, heartache, and extreme disappointment. We may cry out to God repeatedly, asking Him to release us from our troubling circumstances, but not sense His movement on our behalf. He used Joseph's unjust situation to train him for a greater purpose.

One day he became a leader over his brothers. His dream came true, but not until Joseph had been broken and humbled and disciplined. When we are ready for God's blessings, He opens the doors. Up to that point, He calls us to wait in attentive, humble obedience.

If someone is envious of something you have, you probably do not know what that person is feeling. The same is true if you find that you are jealous of another person. Your friend or business associate may never know that you are burning inside with feelings of envy and jealousy. However, God knows. He is aware of the division both feelings create in our hearts and within our relationships.

YOUR SITUATION FROM GOD'S PERSPECTIVE

Jealousy starts inside us—usually with a thought or a feeling that another person has more than we do. Our first inclination is to deny its existence: "I'm not really jealous." Deep inside, however, we look for ways to undermine the other person. We may accomplish this through shutting this person out of our lives or working to turn others against him or her. There is a simple principle we must not forget: we reap what we sow, more than we sow, and later than we sow.

The earmarks of jealousy include the following:

Comparison. We notice a friend or coworker who has something we want. We tell ourselves, "I wish I had her talent, gift, or beauty." Or we see the ability that God has given another person and think, *Lord, You have not done this for me.* God knows what we need and what we can handle. He may want to bless us in a certain area, but if He knows we are not ready for the blessing, He will withhold it for a later time.

His goal is for everyone to be successful, yet success may not come within our time frame. It could come five years from now. And when it does come, it may look completely different from what we imagined. If this is the case, are you willing to wait?

When the enemy tempts you to compare your ability or life to another, refuse to do it. Turn to the Lord in prayer, and ask Him to help you see your life from His perspective. You will be amazed at what you see. Though you feel you are insignificant, you are the apple of His eye. Though you wonder whether you are doing a good job, He knows the faithfulness stored up in your heart, and He is blessed by your life. Though there are times when you may feel that you have very little, you actually have great wealth because God does not limit His blessings to material possessions and bank accounts. The love of our families and the valued relationships we share with friends are greater blessings than anything money could buy.

Therefore, stop rushing, running, and struggling to gain more. If you consider God's personal love for you, you will realize there is nothing more valuable than this.

Competition. Once you compare yourself to another person, you're one step closer to the trip wire and are about to detonate a landmine. Whether it is on the job or in your neighborhood, a competitive attitude can breed anxiety, depression, and hopelessness because it tempts you to ask, *Am I as good as or even better than him or her?* The question you really need to ask is, *Am I doing my best?*

Your best will look differently from that of another person. You may never win an award on earth, but you already have the greater reward—the love of God living within you. You have His Spirit, and you can do much more than you think when your heart and mind are set on pleasing Him and not yourself.

I have discovered that when we focus on having more, gaining more, or receiving more, we begin to lose our sense of peace. We become entangled in the world's thought process. In other words, we stop seeing life from God's viewpoint. This is when we begin to worry about our status. We work harder and longer to achieve goals that God never meant for us to chase. We end up exhausted and weary because we are not living in step with Him. We are living with only our self-made goals in mind.

Fear. A jealous person is fearful of being replaced by somebody or something. This is the nature of jealousy and envy. It is very destructive because it draws us off the course that God has planned for us to travel. When we drift and get into areas that He did not instruct us to enter, we step on landmines and end up wounded emotionally.

If God gives you something but does not give me the same thing, what should I do? Many people complain to God, which creates a conflict within their hearts. It is a conflict—not just with the person who is the object of their jealousy, but also with the Lord. If I am in disagreement with God, then I am in sin.

Strife and dissension are two of the devil's favorite weapons for war. He wants us to be at odds with God and others. He loves to whisper words of jealousy and condemnation. This is why jealousy is so dangerous. It implies that we are not happy with what God has given us. It is one of Satan's favorite weapons, and he knows if he can hook us with it, we will move away from God.

Have you ever considered that the time you spend comparing what someone else has versus what you have is nothing but wasted time? It is. The solution to jealousy is not to deny it, because you can never defeat envy and resentment on your own. It is found in admitting it to the Lord, asking Him to forgive you, and then praying that He would help you to see your life from His perspective.

You may think, *I don't want to admit it, but I wish I was as beautiful as the woman next door,* or *I feel frustrated because I want to sing the lead part in the musical, but the director keeps overlooking my talent.* God really does not want us to compare ourselves to anyone else. The reason is simple: it leads to competition, and this results in fear of losing control. We become anxious or worried and often have trouble with our thoughts and emotions. Many people in our world are struggling with feelings of depression, and so much of it could be avoided if only they would rest in God's providential care. I know there are clinical reasons for some depression, but far too often the anxiety and stress people feel come from the overflow of the pressure they place on themselves.

THE TRUTH ABOUT THE LANDMINES OF JEALOUSY AND ENVY

The consequences of jealousy and envy are deadly. I'm sure that all of us know what it feels like to come upon a yellow jacket nest in the late summer. These fast-moving wasps are relentless. Disturb their nest, which is usually located in the ground, and you will never be able to outrun them. And they know exactly how to focus their energy. In a similar way, if you step on a landmine of jealousy or envy, you will have an entire nest of consequences coming toward you, and you will feel as though there is no escape route.

A critical spirit. Jealousy breeds sin, and it also is a direct pathway to cynicism. People who become jealous at the mention of another's success or something a friend has received are usually very negative. They look for ways to undermine the efforts of others.

Years ago, I had a very dear friend whom I trusted greatly. Another person came on the scene, and almost overnight he stepped into my friend's life and drew him away. The other person was very critical of me, and it was not long before my friend began to believe what was being said. While I made up my mind not to become angry or jealous of the new relationship that was being formed between this man and my former friend, I remember feeling hurt. At that point, I realized I had a choice to make. I could become competitive and critical, or I could trust God with my emotions and the situation. While the other person just "moved in" and stole my friend, I said nothing. His jealousy undermined our friendship, and I had the distinct feeling their relationship would not continue. Before too long, my suspicions came true.

The man who broke up our friendship turned around and dropped my friend. Jealousy had hit its mark. The enemy may have thought that he achieved his goal, but he didn't, because I did not allow jealousy to fill my heart. We need to be on guard at all times for feelings of jealousy even when we come under attack and wonder what God will do on our behalf.

A divided mind. If you are jealous, you will not be able to focus clearly. In fact, you will be distracted. You may have sensed God telling you to go forward in a certain direction. Instead of moving out to do His will, you linger, wondering who is going to get the next assignment. However, your goal needs to be to do the work God has given you. When you do, you will experience His blessings in a tremendous way.

Anger, bitterness, and resentfulness. You can only suppress bitterness so long. In fact, you cannot keep it hidden very long. This is because attitudes like bitterness and jealousy are written in the eyes. If we look closely, we can see joy and happiness on the face of a person who is truly content. Likewise, there usually will be a sense of tenseness or a distance within the eyes of those who allow these feelings to gather within their lives. Anger and bitterness are written on a person's countenance. How do we know this? The author of Proverbs wrote, "The north wind brings forth rain, / And a backbiting tongue, an angry countenance" (25:23). We cannot hide resentfulness. We may try, but sooner or later, it will be revealed to those around us. These will be reflected one way or the other. Before Cain murdered his brother Abel, God asked him, "Why are you angry? And why has your countenance fallen?" (Gen. 4:6). Essentially Cain stepped on the landmine of jealousy, and it exploded beneath him as he killed Abel (v. 8).

A sense of insecurity. Jealousy changes the object of our focus. We become insecure, wondering whether we have done the right thing. When Jesus walked to the disciples on the Sea of Galilee during a horrendous storm, He wanted them to fix their gazes on one thing, and that was Him. The moment we begin to think about who is getting ahead of us, we set ourselves up for trouble.

It is important to be the best you can be at work, in relationships, and in church or civic projects, but you should never forget you are living on God's timeline within His economy. He has a plan to bless you, but first you must learn to follow Him.

The wrong focus. Focus is a key element to living the Christian life successfully. When dog trainers work with animals that will be used as service dogs, they teach the animals a command called "watch." Before the dog receives a command, the trainer will say, "Watch." At that point, the animal will look up and wait for the trainer's next command. It may be wait, heel, or stay. Regardless, the dog's focus is set only on one thing, and that is the trainer.

Whatever has your focus also has you. Ask yourself, *Are the eyes of my heart set on Jesus Christ, or am I angry and jealous of others?* Remember, James wrote, "Where jealousy and selfish ambition exist, there is disorder and every evil thing" (James 3:16). Where there is disorder, there is frustration, anxiety, strife, and other negative feelings.

Sometimes an envious person will seek ways to ruin the reputation of another in order to get ahead. When we step out of God's will by becoming jealous, we also take a step away from His protective care. He has a plan for our lives, but we are determined to head off in another direction. He allows us to travel our own path until we realize we are trapped in a minefield set to explode.

Indecisiveness. In the back of your mind, you may constantly think about the person who seems to have more or know more than you. Regardless of whether this is true or not, focusing on your feelings can be very disrupting. When you are not operating within the guidelines of God's principles, you will not know the right thing to do. More than likely, you will do what you think seems best according to your outlook.

Many believers take one wrong turn after another because they think they are on the right track. They see others headed in a certain direction, and they want to go that way too. God tells us to follow only Him. We learn to do this through prayer and meditation on His Word. When our hearts are submitted to Him, the Holy Spirit will guide and direct our path—a path that leads to many blessings.

Struggle with feelings of depression. When you open the door to jealousy, you also open the door to a host of other difficulties, such as feelings of despair and depression. I am not suggesting that you will become clinically depressed. However, depression usually comes when we deliberately invite sin into our lives.

For example, you may be at odds with a coworker or friend, and the first thing you do in the morning is begin to think about that person. You wonder if he is getting ahead of you. All day long you are stewing inside over the fact that you do not have what he has. God instructs us to "cease striving and know that [He is] God" (Ps. 46:10). Actually no one knows what others are facing—the heartaches and difficulties.

As you think about this person and try to manipulate your circumstances to get ahead of him, you become more anxious and downcast. The psalmist told us to lift our eyes to the Lord because He is our help and strength (Ps. 121:1). This is exactly what cures a jealous heart, a depressed mind, and an anxious spirit. When you come to the place where you realize the great love and affection that God has for you, you will not be worried about what others have. You will just want God's best given to you exactly when and how He plans the delivery.

A loss of privileges and opportunities. Jealousy positions us for a crash in our emotions as well as our professional lives. When there is no peace, contentment, or happiness within our hearts, others will have a hard time working alongside us. When others sense that we are jealous or envious, they will make note of this and steer clear. We may find ourselves wondering what we have done, but the answer is clear to those who have listened to our conversation.

Broken fellowship with God. You can read your Bible and pray, but something will be missing because there will be a wall between you and the Lord. This is because jealousy is a self-centered emotion. Instead of having a grateful heart for what God has given, we spend time thinking about what others have or what we wish we had. Fellowship with God becomes a second, third, or last choice.

In some cases, a jealous person cannot pray with true devotion because she only wants to ask God to deal with "the other person." And the other person may be someone He has chosen to bless. Remember what I said in the beginning: Satan's goal is to bring destruction into your life. He wants to distract you and prevent you from serving God with a whole heart, and jealousy is just one entrapment that he plans along your pathway.

Physical sickness. Bitterness, resentment, hostility, anger, jealousy, and envy can be stepping-stones to physical disease. Most of our lives we have heard people talk about having something "eat away" at them on the inside. The outcropping of jealousy is anger, and this can result in a list of physical problems. When your heart is right with God, you will be healthier. The writer of Proverbs noted, "A joyful heart is good medicine, / But a broken spirit dries up the bones" (17:22). In other words, the entire body is affected by the inner turmoil we fuel through sinful thoughts and actions.

DISARMING JEALOUSY

How do we effectively deal with the jealousy in our own lives?

First, we need to admit that we are envious. When we find ourselves in conflict with someone we believe has more than we do, we need to acknowledge it to the Lord in prayer.

Second, we need to acknowledge that we are in conflict with God. As long as we think we can patch up the situation, camouflage it, or rationalize it, we won't deal with the true issue, which is a heart full of envy. However, when we willingly admit that there is a problem and that we need God's help, our hearts are open to receive His instruction. Once this takes place, we usually notice that while feelings of jealousy may linger, they soon begin to fade.

If there is a chance you are jealous of another person, ask God to help you find a way to encourage, compliment, or befriend that individual. The enemy is not the person at the center of your jealousy. It is Satan with his cruel desire to entrap you in sin and blow up your life with feelings of envy. But godly repentance and submission to God defuse his traps. Not only are you freed from his entanglement, but you suddenly realize that God has so much more in store for your life—just because He loves you with an everlasting love.

Third, we need to thank God for what He has done in our lives and even for the people who are the source of our conflict. Doing this may seem difficult, but acknowledge your problem, confess it, and thank Him for revealing this struggle in your life.

Praise Him for the good things He has given you. Resist the temptation to compare yourself to anyone else. Also, eliminate ungodly negative feelings, because they often do not reflect the truth. You may feel someone has hurt you, but God wants you not to hold a grudge or seek revenge. Both of these create deep hostility within our hearts. Remember, the cure to jealousy resides within us as well because our lives contain God's Spirit. He is the only One who can truly help us discern when feelings of jealousy arise. Therefore, ask Him to help you see your life from His perspective, brimming with hope and blessing. Once you grasp the good plans He has for you, jealousy will no longer be a landmine in your life.

Fourth, we need to pray and ask God to help us see the heart of the other person at the center of the conflict. Jealousy is everywhere—the corporate world, the ministry, the government, politics, your office, and even your neighborhood. You may be jealous of someone who is just being the person God has created her to be. When another person is living God's plan, we never have an excuse to be envious of her.

There is no way for you to know all that another person is facing. He could be dealing with some hurtful situation that is causing him to act a certain way. Instead of joining in on the push to get ahead, ask God to help you rest in His presence. When you learn to sit before Him, waiting for His timing and His direction, you will receive a blessing.

Fifth, we need to be willing to wait for God to work. Times of waiting offer wonderful opportunities for us to grow closer to the Lord. As we wait, we also can listen for His voice of instruction teaching us how to live a life that is successful, whether this includes building friendships, working alongside others, or developing new hobbies. Along with waiting comes the need to be open to God's guidance and ready to obey Him at all times in every situation.

Sixth, we need to ask God to help us hear His voice over the clamor of the world. Jealousy shouts for attention. Thoughts of envy try to creep into the forefront of your mind. Therefore, stand firm in your desire to hear God's voice and know His mind for your life and situation.

Seventh, we need to delight ourselves in God (Ps. 37:4). When we do, we will find that He will give us the desires of our hearts.

SURRENDER LEADS TO VICTORY

How do you handle the jealousy of another person toward you? The best way is to surrender your feelings to God and allow Him to change your attitude toward others.

First, you need to ask God to show you what you need to learn through this situation. This requires being willing to lay down your own will and desires. Many times people become jealous not because of something we have done but because they feel inadequate or they can never measure up to the standards of those around them. Before a jealous person irritates you, be willing to pray for him, and ask God to help you understand how you can serve that individual rather than shun him.

Second, you need to make a conscious decision to ignore any harsh words that have been spoken as a result of jealous feelings. Once again, surrender any rights you think you have to Christ. Allow Him to defend you and also to take care of your reputation. All of us want to know that our lives count for something. People also become jealous as a result of feelings of worthlessness. You may not be able to speak truth to a person who is struggling with this landmine, but you certainly can refuse to take a wrong turn—a turn that could lead to destruction.

Third, ask God to show you if there is something that you have done to create an atmosphere of jealousy. More than likely, Joseph enjoyed showing off the coat his father had given to him. Jealousy filled his brothers' hearts, and even though their actions were not justified, we can see how Joseph's actions helped to trigger the landmine.

Fourth, show the person who is struggling with jealousy some form of kindness. Kindness is a powerful tool. Compliment her. For example, say something like this: "I was so excited to hear about your promotion." Or make a point to help her in some way. The other person may never know what you have done or may never care. However, God sees your good intentions, and He will bless you, not just for your act of kindness, but for the change in the attitude of your heart.

Fifth, pray for your attitude to be changed and also for the person involved to focus on the Lord and His purposes instead of seeking to bring disunity to the lives of others. Sometimes, if another person is jealous of you, then the moment you begin to talk with him, you can feel the walls go up. No one needs to become a doormat for others, but we certainly need to allow God to use us and teach us how to have humble, pliable hearts for Him.

How should you deal with jealousy? Keep your heart focused on the Lord. Whenever you feel a twinge of jealousy, you need to be honest and go to Him in prayer, asking for His help in dealing with it. You also need to confess jealousy as sin, repent, and turn away from it. From time to time, each one of us will face temptation in this area and the others mentioned in this book. However, we do not have to yield to any of the deadly landmines the enemy places in our path. Don't allow him or anyone to tempt you into disobeying God. You have been created for a purpose, and that is to glorify the Lord. When you walk through life in step with His principles, you will never be sorry. In fact, life will be fantastic because you will experience His blessings at every turn.

FIVE

THE LANDMINE OF INSECURITY

Imagine for a moment the scene where Moses is standing at the burning bush. He is overwhelmed by the power and magnitude of God's holy presence. For forty years he had lived a humble existence in Midian—a land on the edge of the desert bordering Gilead, Edom, and Moab—with his extended family, who were mostly shepherds. The memory of his departure from Egypt forty years earlier was still very fresh. He had left suddenly after killing an Egyptian who was mistreating a Hebrew slave.

Now he was standing before the Lord, receiving instruction about how he would live the rest of his life. God's command to Moses required both courage and devotion. He was facing a lifestyle change that also would alter the way he felt about himself and especially the way he viewed God. It was a defining moment of extreme proportions, and like many of us, Moses immediately felt unequal to the task. He wavered in doubt and looked for a way to sidestep the call.

Moses was right: he was not equal to the task! This fact did not change God's plan for his life, however. Most of the challenges we face require faith in an infinite, all-powerful God. Regardless of the task, if we are convinced that we cannot succeed, we won't. On the other hand, if we trust the sovereignty and strength of God at work in our lives, we will succeed.

EXPOSING THE TRUTH ABOUT INSECURITY

God instructed Moses to go to Pharaoh and speak the very words He would give him to say. The Lord was setting the stage for the deliverance of His people. In response Moses cringed at the idea, as most of us would have done. He had grown up in Pharaoh's household. It was there that he discovered the truth concerning his birth. He was a Hebrew—like those who served as Egyptian slaves. How could he possibly go back? What's more, he felt that he was not equipped for the task God was asking him to do.

Have you ever felt this way? You know the Lord has led you to a certain point. He has placed you in a position that requires more of you than you believe you can do. How do you answer Him? As Moses gave his reply, we can hear the insecurity in his voice: "Please, Lord, I have never been eloquent . . . for I am slow of speech and slow of tongue" (Ex. 4:10). Insecurity is not a struggle like jealousy, envy, or pride. It may not sound explosive, but it is. The landmine of insecurity is both dangerous and destructive. To a person with a sense of insecurity, everything within her life seems unstable and unreliable.

You may have been given the opportunity to move ahead in your job, but you want to refuse the promotion because you do not believe that you can do the work or that you will be accepted. Moses could not imagine going to Pharaoh with God's message and saying, "Let my people go."

God in His faithfulness reassured Moses that He would be with him every step of the way, and the same is true for you and me when we are walking in the Lord's will. "The LORD said to [Moses], 'Who has made man's mouth? Or who makes him mute or deaf, or seeing or blind? Is it not I, the LORD? Now then go, and I, even I, will be with your mouth, and teach you what you are to say'" (Ex. 4:11–12). It would have been nice if Moses had accepted God's call without a conditional clause, but he didn't. He did not believe he could lead God's people out of Egypt alone. The Lord knew Moses would have a hard time answering the call. Therefore, He suggested that Aaron become a vital part of the plan. Aaron's involvement was not a part of His original plan. In this case, Aaron would be the one who would speak the words Moses told him to say. And those words came straight from the Lord.

The result was obedience, with Moses answering the call even though he did not fully think he could do what God was calling him to do. God knows our limitations and usually will place us in situations that stretch our faith beyond what we think we can bear. He wants to develop our faith. In order to do this, faith must be tested. This means placing us in situations where we must come face-to-face with our insecurities and where we choose to trust God with the situation.

At some point, you probably have felt like Moses. An opportunity has opened before you, but you did not think that you could handle the responsibility. Everything within you wanted to run away, but you also felt the Holy Spirit urging you to stay and give it your best try. Paul told us in Ephesians, "We are His workmanship, created in Christ Jesus for good works, which God prepared beforehand so that we would walk in them" (2:10).

You may think, *I can't do anything well*, but from God's perspective, you are a person of notable excellence. You can do all things through Christ (Phil. 4:13). Moses had to learn that truth, as did Paul and everyone who chooses to follow the ways of God. He never leaves us in situations of mediocrity. He wants to challenge us to reach greater goals than we thought possible. In a short period of time, Moses went from being a shepherd to the leader of the Exodus. That was quite a shift in roles, and God just may do a similar work in your life, but first you must be willing to trust and obey Him.

TAKE THE RIGHT STEPS TO AVOID INSECURITY

Do you feel good about yourself, or do you often engage in self-criticism? What is there about yourself that you do not like? Maybe it is the way you look. Far too often, we see people on television and begin to think that our lives just don't add up. We don't look handsome, pretty, or fashionable. Our self-esteem suffers because we are comparing ourselves to others who are living for the world and its passions and not for God. How do you conquer feelings of low self-esteem, especially when you have believed Satan's lie telling you that you are not capable or worthy of God's blessings?

First, you need to remember that Satan will stop at nothing to lay landmines of insecurity within your life. He wants you to drop back with feelings of insecurity. He knows God has a plan for you. Satan also is aware of your potential because of the presence of God's Spirit. Therefore, he enjoys setting little explosions of insecurity throughout your life with the hope of them turning into a blaze of discouragement and hopelessness. You can detect and defuse his enticements.

You have an awesome opportunity to have a personal relationship with the God of the universe. It is not a matter of just knowing about Him. You can actually know Him and experience His eternal, unconditional love. From time to time, everyone struggles with feelings of insecurity. You may have to speak to a group of people and wonder if what you have said or done was correct, effective, or thought provoking.

However, it is one thing to feel insecure about a particular situation and another thing to grow up with insecurity and have it programmed into your thinking every day. Insecure thoughts can isolate you from others. I have heard many people at the end of their lives express a desire to turn back time and change the way they lived. Most say they would have made different decisions at key times. Satan's intent with insecurity is to leave us feeling disappointed and more like failures than conquerors, but we must remember that we are more than conquerors through Christ (Rom. 8:37).

THE ROOT CAUSES OF INSECURITY

What causes someone to feel insecure? Many times this comes as a result of feeling inadequate. At some point, she may have faced rejection or a lack of acceptance. Each one of us has struggles with feelings of insecurity. There will be times when you wake up in the morning and feel as though you have no sense of direction. You may wonder what the future holds. Deep inside there is a churning that does not stop, and you may ask yourself, *Will I ever be content?* If you have a sense of security in God, then you will discover the peace and joy that He has to offer no matter what your situation may be.

Broken relationships can leave us wondering if we have a character flaw. Or facing a layoff at work can leave a person feeling insecure about the future as well as his personal ability. Growing older and realizing you may not reach the goals you wanted to reach can have a disastrous effect. Losing a loved one can revive or create feelings of insecurity, fear, and depression. There are numerous causes of insecurity, but God wants us to know that we are secure in Him. We do not have to fear the future or be concerned about what another person may think of us (Rom. 8:38–39).

Feeling threatened, off balance, or on the edge. One of the primary reasons some people feel insecure is because they grew up in an insecure environment. Their world seemed very unpredictable, and there was an uncertainty to life that prevented them from feeling safe.

They may feel off balance because their father was an alcoholic or their mother or father left home or died when they were young. These situations create an atmosphere of instability. Just when a child needs to know that he or she is safe, loved, and cared for, the bottom to life seems to drop out. Often the child grows up to be an adult with deep-seated insecurities.

The loss of a parent is one of the most devastating events that can take place in a child's life. It can easily shake the emotional foundation of her world. I meet people who tell me that years ago—when they were young—their mother or father died and they have never recovered from this loss. They still have a sense of emptiness and insecurity that they cannot shake.

There are other circumstances that create instability in our lives— *failure, a financial loss,* or *divorce.* When we feel insecure about ourselves, we will not be able to accomplish the goals that God has set for us to reach. The reason this happens is that we feel inadequate, inferior, and insecure. Like Moses, we will want God to "send someone else" or to send someone to help us with the task. We'll try to hide in the back of the crowd, hoping that no one will notice us. But God always does. He knows our potential—the same way He knew the potential of Moses. He does not want us to feel insecure; He wants us to trust Him. When we do, we will gain a sense of security because God supports us with an unshakable sense of power.

Having unrealistic rules and regulations can stifle the natural creativity that God has placed within us. Sometimes parents set rules that they could not keep. Though children cannot know the breadth of the consequences, they must know deep inside that the regulation is too great or difficult for them to handle. The frustration created by this inner conflict can lead to deep-seated feelings of inadequacy. Rules are meant to help us live according to God's will and plan. However, far too often, they are misused in an effort to confine and thus prevent a child or young adult from trusting and believing in God's sovereign ability.

Rules certainly give us boundaries to live by, but they need to have purpose and meaning. For example, if you require your son or daughter to make straight A's when your child is capable of bringing home only Bs and Cs, then the pressure and drive to do more will create a sense of inadequacy deep within that young person. You always need to do your best, look your best, and be your best. However, if your best is set at a certain level, you need to ask God to help you to accept this. Often, a person may feel jealous because she has compared herself to someone else. Instead of thanking God for the ability He has given her, she feels threatened and insecure because she wants more than He has provided at this point.

Each one of us needs to learn to have a grateful heart for what has been given to us. When you thank God for the things He has provided, your insecurity level drops and your security in Him increases because you begin to see Him as He is—the source of your every need. Always set a goal to do your best, but also make it a priority to ask God to give you His ability while exposing any insecurity you may face. Many people live below their potential because they have settled for less. They feel insecure and stop. The way to overcome this is to

- ask God to help you see your life from His perspective.

- be willing to obey Him and grow in your knowledge about Him and His way.

- seek to be a success from God's viewpoint and not from the world's standard.

Also, setting unrealistic goals that God does not want you to establish can lead to insecure feelings, especially for young children. These can create a sense of frustration and tension within their lives that can lead to insecurity. Instead of growing up believing that he can reach his greatest potential, a child may think the opposite: *I'm no good. I'm not worthy. I can't do anything right.* Parents need to set godly principles for their children to follow.

When we follow His ways, our children will have a healthy, strong self-esteem that will not be undermined by the negativity of this world.

You may take a moment to ask yourself the following question: *Am I requiring more of my son or daughter than I do of myself?* Setting realistic goals and boundaries for your family creates an atmosphere of obedience and success. We also need to follow this principle for our lives. Some people demand more of themselves than God does of them. The result is one series of failures after another. For example, He may never have planned for you to be a senior vice president of a company, but you keep pushing and pushing. Inside, you are fighting feelings of inadequacy. Your relationship with your spouse is suffering because all you can think about is how you want to be at the top of the corporate ladder or that you would like to become president of the parent-teacher organization at your son's elementary school.

In the end, most of the people who are on the top probably would tell you the strife and the frustration it took to get there were not worth the struggle. Along the way, personal relationships suffered, and in some cases, lifelong friendships dissolved. Friendship and family are the very things God uses to encourage us and build security within our lives. Usually, however, these are the very things that suffer most whenever we are pushing past everyone else. Our struggle with insecurity drives us to be more, but it also leaves a fearful aftertaste of insecurity within our emotions that prevents us from becoming all that God wants us to be.

What does He have to say about insecurity? That it is deadly, and if Satan has his way, he will use it to prevent us from accomplishing the goals God wants us to reach in our lifetimes.

Having a poor body image. After you watch some of the commercials on television, it may seem that few people are happy with the way they look. Either we think we are too skinny or too overweight. Those who are short want to be taller, and the ones who are tall think, *If only I could be shorter!*

This line of thinking and rethinking can lead to insecurity. Regardless of your shape or size, God sees one thing when He looks at you—the person He loves and the one He created with an awesome sense of potential. You do not have to be the leader of the pack to have His approval.

Not receiving positive feedback. Perhaps while you were growing up, you did not have a father or a mother who encouraged you or gave you positive feedback. No one ever told you, "I know you did your best, and I'm proud of you." When people do not receive the right kind of praise and encouragement, there is a strong chance they will develop a negative self-image. They also will find it hard to believe that God really loves them and accepts them unconditionally. Satan capitalizes, and places an enormous landmine of insecurity. Without God's help, it will explode.

My mother always encouraged me to do my best. She knew that I had enough obstacles to overcome as a result of growing up without a father. If I told her, "Mom, I did the best I could do," she would say, "It's okay." She believed in me and understood that God had a plan for my life that went beyond anything she personally desired at that moment. Trust is a key factor in training and mentoring children. If she had scolded me and chided me to do more than I could do, I'm convinced her words would have had a very damaging effect on me. She didn't do that. Instead, she loved me, talked with me, listened to my heart, and prayed with and for me.

The temptation to feel inadequate was already present due to my father's untimely death. However, her encouragement brought focus and stability to my young life. God also used this to motivate me to be the very best I could be. Later, God's acceptance and approval motivated me to be successful in all that He called me to do. Yet without the foundational love and acceptance given to me by my mother, life may have been very different for me.

Being overshadowed by siblings. We don't know for sure, but David probably struggled with feelings of insecurity. After all, his brothers reminded him how unimportant his life seemed because he was tending only a few sheep (1 Sam. 17:28) The truth was, God was in the process of preparing him for a tremendous blessing. And the same is true of you. It doesn't matter if you are six or eighty-six. The moment you confess your sense of insecurity to God and your need of Him, He begins to work on your behalf.

Train your heart and mind to focus on Him and not only on your circumstances. As I mentioned earlier, whatever has your attention has you. Therefore, don't allow negative feelings to control your life and keep you from achieving all that God has for you to achieve and experience.

In prison, Joseph focused on the Lord and the dream He had given him and not the fact that his brothers had caused his pain and suffering. God allowed him to face great hardship for an even greater purpose. You don't have to feel inadequate any longer. No one is adequate apart from God. He is the source of our strength and our sufficiency. The apostle Paul wrote, "I can do all things through Him who strengthens me" (Phil. 4:13).

Joseph didn't seek to push his way to the front of any line to win release. He waited patiently for God's deliverance. During his time of confinement, he learned how to be the best he could be at that moment. The same is true of David's life. Both men, and in fact all of the godly people mentioned in the Bible that the Lord used, faced horrendous circumstances. Yet they made a choice to trust God and leave the consequences to Him. They refused to become entangled by negative thoughts.

God uses our circumstances to shape us. If He allows difficulties, then you know He is going to do something wonderful in your life. If you grew up hearing how much smarter your brother or sister was, then you probably felt insecure and frustrated. God will never compare you to another person. You are His, and He loves you just the way you are. If you trust Him, He will teach you all you need to know, and in His book, you will never see a failing grade.

First, you must believe in His ability and faithfulness. Second, you must trust Him even when the odds seem stacked against you. And third, you must be willing to wait for His timing. When you do, you will receive a great blessing. There is something reassuring about offering hope to another person. Instead of tearing someone down, look for ways to lift others up and encourage them to keep going and not fall prey to insecurity.

The insecure person often says, "The only reason you are being nice to me is that you want something." He can't believe that someone would be nice without wanting something in return.

When we grasp the depth of God's love for us, we won't be afraid to open our hearts to others. There are people who have been so deeply hurt they forgo building relationships rather than risk being hurt again.

Just like the other struggles mentioned in this book, you can disarm insecurity, but to do this you must admit you have a problem: "Lord, I feel insecure. I'm not suited for the task." Therefore, you think, *I can't accept the job offer. I can't take that risk because I will fail. I will never reach that goal. I'm a failure. No one loves me.*

These are the enemy's landmines that he places in the pathway of the believer. Whenever you listen to his voice instead of the voice of truth that comes from God's Spirit within, you set yourself up for failure. You do not have to live with a sense of insecurity. Never let anyone tell you that you cannot reach the goals God helps you set. And do not listen to the words of others that say, "You are inadequate. You can't do this job." More important, do not allow negative thoughts or words to define who you are as a child of God. God wants you to remember that you are more than adequate through Christ who gives

75

you the strength and wisdom to face each day (Phil. 4:13). You have everything you need to become what God has created you to be.

The human imagination is powerful. If you have godly dreams hidden within your heart, then ask Him to bring them to the forefront and help you reach each one. God is the One who gives us the ability to set goals and dream good things for the future. A young man may feel called into the ministry, but he doesn't feel as though he can follow through on this dream because he grew up thinking that he is not smart. God gives us many dreams we hold within our hearts. He is not limited in power, and if we will offer ourselves to Him, He will give us exactly what we need to accomplish our goals.

Don't miss His blessings because you think you can't do it. When He opens a door, step through it, and trust Him to help you learn, grow, and accomplish the goals He helps you set. Jesus told His disciples, "All things you ask in prayer, believing, you will receive" (Matt. 21:22). This is a conditional promise because it is based on faith—our faith in God to answer our prayers.

Jesus didn't say, "Listen, I know you guys mean well, but you don't have the education it takes to get ahead in this world. You just need to hang back and let others pass by you." No, He said *believe* as if there is no doubt because the same God Who loves you unconditionally will lead and guide your every step.

He will never give you more than you can handle, and if He gives you an opportunity, He also will empower you to do the work. Never once will He leave you alone to fight life's battles. He is faithful and true, and you can trust Him fully (Rev. 19:11). Believe because "all things are possible to him who believes" (Mark 9:23).

There are some things we will not be able to do because God has not called us to do them. However, there are other things that He wants us to do. We will face feelings of insecurity and even feel as though we cannot do the task, but we can through Him. Too many people see a challenge and immediately think, *I know I can't do it, so I won't even try.*

Thomas Edison failed more than a thousand times in his attempt to create a lightbulb, but he never gave up. Think what would have happened if he had said, "Candles are good enough." He never would have reached his goal. Someone else would have created the lightbulb, and he would have missed a tremendous opportunity. Though he faced one disappointment after another, Edison stayed the course, and that made the difference. He did not give up or cave in to thoughts of insecurity.

If you quit, you will never know just how close you are to success. It could be a matter of one more try. At some point, everyone who tries will fail. But often, it is in the times of failure that God does His greatest work. He uses each one of our failures to mold our lives so we will become the people He has planned for us to be. When trouble or disappointment comes, imagine what would happen if you asked, "Lord, show me Your will in all of this. What do You want me to learn personally from this time of heartache and trouble?" An insecure person may think, *God doesn't have a plan for my life. There is no way He cares about me.* He does care, and He also has a plan for your life (Jer. 29:11).

SET YOUR FOCUS ON CHRIST AND RECEIVE THE VICTORY

Don't allow your mind to be programmed with negative thoughts that lead to insecurity. I have heard people say, "I am just dumb." No, you are not. The same God who created the universe—along with every living thing in it—created you. He gave you life, and He has a plan that only you can fulfill. You are not a failure or a loser; you are not incompetent. You need to reprogram your thinking with His truth by exposing the landmine hidden within your life. Then you need to change the way you think and talk about yourself.

You are a child of God, and He wants you to learn to view your life from His perspective. You may think, *I'll never be a success.* But you already are in His eyes. He loves you unconditionally and wants you to live up to your full potential. Thank Him for your life and for the work He is going to do as you trust Him with your insecurities.

God has given us powerful principles to apply to our lives. He doesn't want us believing Satan's lies that tell us we need to live by chance. There is no such thing as chance or luck in the life of a believer. He knows everything that takes place, and nothing we face is greater than His sovereignty. As children of God, we are living under the canopy of His blessings. Therefore, we are not losers. We are people of great worth because of Jesus Christ.

Some people are so insecure that they believe if they just try harder, they can earn God's love. But they can't. God has given us all of Himself and all of His love on Calvary's cross. There is no greater form of love and acceptance than what has been given to you by God through the life and death and resurrection of His Son. The Cross is the greatest statement of love and security that has ever been made or will be made.

No one could love you more than Jesus. He loves you—your hair, your eyes, your laughter, your tears, and your smile—all of you. And even more than this, He believes in you. You cannot disappoint Him, because He knows all about you—your sins and failures—and yet He died for you so that you could come to know Him as Savior and Lord and everlasting Friend. What more could we ask to receive than love so great and divine?

How could you possibly lose while living your life for Him? There is absolutely no way. He never changes in His affection for you: He is the same today, tomorrow, and forever. The apostle Paul told us that He has "set his seal of ownership on us, and put his Spirit in our hearts as a deposit, guaranteeing what is to come. . . . It is by faith you stand firm" (2 Cor. 1:22, 24 NIV).

When we accept Christ as our Savior, God places a seal of ownership on our lives. In the Bible, the word *seal* often was used metaphorically as an expression of something that was held securely. God has given us a seal—the Holy Spirit—as a guarantee of His eternal love. Whenever we feel insecure or tempted to give up, all we need to do is to turn to Him in prayer, and He will provide the hope we need to continue.

I remember a time when a group at church opposed me and did not want me to continue as pastor. The temptation that came to me was one of worry, fear, and insecurity. I instantly knew that if I listened to these voices, I would not be able to hear God's voice. Therefore, instead of giving in to thoughts of fear, I sought God in prayer, asking for His wisdom and encouragement.

While I was in a meeting upstairs in the church, another group was downstairs seeking a way to remove me as pastor. As those around me talked through the things that were happening, I remember being focused on only one thing: God's will. At that moment, He reminded me of the words in Isaiah 54:17, "No weapon that is formed against you will prosper; / And every tongue that accuses you in judgment you will condemn."

These words contained a powerful message of confidence and hope. It was also a warning in a sense not to give up or give in to fear. The enemy has one goal for the child of God, and that is destruction through any means he can use. He will tempt us to feel insecure, hopeless, abandoned, forgotten, and misused. His words are always laced with discouragement and accusations. Don't fall for his schemes. If others speak badly about you, keep your heart set on Christ. Do your best and trust Him to be your rear guard (Isa. 52:12; 58:8).

DISCOVERING GOD'S GOODNESS AND OVERCOMING INSECURITY

When we start to live the life God intended for us, we will face opposition. The enemy is not going to give up and walk away quietly. He wants us to feel really bad about ourselves so we will give up and no longer approach each day with a sense of excitement and hope. He will even use other believers to tempt us into thinking that we are not good enough. Careless words spoken or flashes of anger can leave us feeling defeated, especially if we grew up in environments where we were told that we would never accomplish anything in life.

God wants you to stop viewing your life from the world's perspective. He wants to set you free from the bondage of insecurity and help you to be the person He has created you to be. This may be difficult for some who grew up in a negative home environment. It may take time to reprogram your thinking, but God will give you the opportunity to do this, and you must be willing to trust Him.

Therefore, when negative thoughts enter your mind, ask Him to help you imagine His best—His thoughts and the good things concerning His nature and personal love for you. For example, when you feel unloved, recall His truth: He loves you unconditionally. He will never leave or forsake you. He will give you the strength you need according to His riches in glory. He is mindful of your every need and will provide for each one. Nothing is too difficult for Him, and no matter what happens, He will never deny loving and knowing you. He is yours and you are His—forever!

What are the effects of insecurity?

- a lack of lasting relationships
- a perception of being prideful or snobbish
- indecisiveness
- a fearful attitude
- a brooding sense of anger
- a record of being passed over for promotions and honors
- the inability to meet others and establish friendships
- the belief that success is based on the praise, approval, and acceptance of others
- the desire to be in charge of every conversation

The greatest effect that insecurity will have on your life concerns your relationship with God. The deeper the insecurity, the more likely you will struggle with your relationship with Him. You can't focus on worshiping Him when your mind is set on yourself—how you appear to others and what you can do to get ahead. The only thing that can bring true, lasting security to your heart is a personal relationship with Jesus Christ. Everything else is secondary and never will bring contentment.

Intimacy, even between friends, requires self-disclosure to greater and lesser degrees. When it comes to knowing God, He wants you to open every area of your life to Him. Then He will show you how much to share with others. If you hold friendships at an arm's length because you feel insecure, you will miss a tremendous blessing—the type of blessing David and Jonathan enjoyed (1 Sam. 20).

Each one of us longs to have friendships. People may say that they are okay being alone, but God did not create us to be isolated from others. He created us for fellowship first with Him and then with other people. How we approach our relationship with Him indicates how we will be in the company of neighbors, coworkers, family members, and other loved ones.

TAKE THE RIGHT STEPS TO OVERCOME INSECURITY

If you are battling insecurity, how do you overcome it? How do you win the victory and begin to live truly free of Satan's negative, self-defeating obstacles? One of the most important steps is to ask God to expose the problem of insecurity. As painful as it may seem, be willing to open up your heart to Him and confess your feelings of low self-esteem. This is the key step to healing, and it is an essential step to gaining God's strength for your situation. As a young man, David had tremendous courage even though his brothers ridiculed him and questioned why he showed up on the battlefield to fight Goliath. A courageous spirit is not something that we receive at birth. We gain courage through faith in God.

When David dared to stand up and volunteer to face the Philistine giant, his oldest brother scoffed at him, saying, "Why have you come down? And with whom have you left those few sheep in the wilderness?" (1 Sam. 17:28). In other words, "You are not equal to the task. Why are you even here? You are not doing anything worthwhile. After all, your chief occupation is just taking care of a few sheep."

Perhaps you have felt the same way. God places a challenge in front of you, and your first thought is, *I can do this!* But then the enemy whispers words of discouragement to your heart. At first he chides you with simple comments. As you continue to move forward to complete the task, he sets landmines of insecurity in your path to explode and cause deep frustration and discouragement.

The Bible tells us, "[David] turned away from [his brother]" (v. 30). You must do the same thing with thoughts of insecurity—turn away from them by turning to face your only true hope—the Lord Jesus Christ.

Concerning his victory over Goliath, David wrote,

> The LORD is my light and my salvation;
> Whom shall I fear?
> The LORD is the defense of my life;
> Whom shall I dread? (Ps. 27:1)

The enemy is relentless in his attack on your mind. If he notices you turning a fearful or insecure ear to listen to his accusations, he will open up a full assault on your emotions until you have collapsed in the dust of disappointment.

When we feel insecure, we feel hopeless, helpless, overwhelmed, and unable to accomplish anything. It involves a feeling of inner turmoil, and that is exactly what the armies of Israel were feeling as they faced the Philistines. That is what Moses struggled with for a brief second in time. The way to overcome insecurity is to anchor your heart, soul, and mind to the unshakable love and power of the living God through faith in Jesus Christ.

David told King Saul, "Let no man's heart fail on account of him [Goliath]; your servant will go and fight with this Philistine" (1 Sam. 17:32). An entire nation was shaking in its boots with insecurity at the sight of this huge warrior, but a young man stepped forward and said to his enemy, "This day the LORD will deliver you up into my hands, and I will strike you down" (v. 46).

You can't enjoy life if you feel insecure. You can't accomplish the goals God has given you if you feel overwhelmed and fearful. And the truth is, God never meant for you to struggle with feelings that lead to defeat. You may not find yourself facing enemies with the physical strength of Goliath, but if you live long enough, sooner or later you will meet the enemies of discouragement, hopelessness, and fear. At some point, each one of us will battle insecurity.

Acknowledge your feelings of insecurity. God already knows exactly what you are feeling, and He has a plan to help you view your life differently—from His perspective, which is one of hope and potential. Ask Him to help you identify your insecurities. Be honest and ask, "What causes me to feel insecure?" Maybe a certain situation brings thoughts of inadequacy. Once you identify the problem area, you can go to work on changing your incorrect beliefs with God's help.

Make the decision to overcome insecurity. If you have never trusted Christ as your Savior, then you will not be able to overcome insecurity. You can work hard to lessen the fallout from this landmine, but you can conquer it only through Christ. It requires a walk of faith with the Savior. Recognizing there is a problem may come quickly, but dealing with the root can take time.

The moment you roll your struggle onto the Lord, you will begin to feel lighter and much more open to the blessings that God has for you. Remember, if you don't set a goal to deal with this, then you will never be free from its entrapment. You must make up your mind to stop hiding behind your insecurity.

Realize that dealing with insecurity involves self-esteem. The way you view yourself is not necessarily the way you are. Too many people see themselves from a negative viewpoint. Some may be prideful and not see the effects of insecurity on their lives. Regardless, to deal correctly with insecurity, you must gain the proper perspective. Ask God to show you how He sees your life. Refuse to focus on the negative.

Instead, focus on the Holy Spirit, who lives inside you. The best way to do this is to immerse yourself in the Word of God. His Word is powerful—"living and active and sharper than any two-edged sword, and piercing as far as the division of soul and spirit, of both joints and marrow, and able to judge the thoughts and intentions of the heart" (Heb. 4:12). When you read what God has to say about you, you gain an entirely different viewpoint. In times of sin, God may discipline you, but He never condemns or belittles you. Therefore, as you study the Scriptures, you begin to think differently and then act differently. Actions always follow what we think.

If you have a negative mind-set, you will have a negative view of life—particularly who you are. God wants you to step away from destructive feelings and thoughts. He has good plans for your life and sees you as a person of tremendous potential because of the life of His Son, Who lives within you.

Focus on positive qualities. Stop the negative self-talk. Even though the odds were stacked against him, David did not hesitate to confront Goliath. Joseph did not lie around in prison complaining that he had been wrongly treated. He surveyed his circumstances from a godly viewpoint and concluded that because of the potential his life contained, he could run the jail if God gave him the opportunity.

That was exactly what happened: "The chief jailer committed to Joseph's charge all the prisoners who were in the jail; so that whatever was done there, he was responsible for it" (Gen. 39:22). Is there something that God wants you to do, but you have held back because of insecurity? He is waiting for you to obey Him and to leave all the consequences to Him. He knows when you are worried and fearful, but He has given you an anchor to your soul—the Lord Jesus Christ, who is your immovable source of strength and comfort. Trust Him. Obey Him and watch God work on your behalf.

Ask God to help you visualize His work in your life. David had to see beyond his circumstances, which included facing a literal killing machine. Goliath's presence intimidated an entire army, but not David. Standing on the brink of the battle, he immediately thought back to the times the Lord gave him the strength to fight a bear and a lion to protect his father's sheep. He had the right attitude because he was focused on the right thing: "I come to you in the name of the LORD of hosts, the God of the armies of Israel, whom you have taunted" (1 Sam. 17:45).

Saul wanted David to use his personal armor and weapons, but David refused. God loves for us to trust Him purely and simply. Goliath was defeated and killed that day by a young boy—a lad who was jeered by his brothers. His choice of weapons—five smooth stones, a sling, and a courageous mind-set. Just to make sure you remember well, David's first stone hit the target. God has a victory waiting for you, but it cannot be won with insecurity.

Stop comparing yourself to others. We talked about this earlier. The moment you compare yourself to another person, you set yourself up for failure. You also derail God's plan to use you in someone else's life. Few, if any of us, can honestly compliment another person while we are feeling insecure about ourselves. When we compare ourselves to others, we usually feel threatened as we battle feelings of insecurity and low self-esteem.

Ask God to show you what He has planned for your life. There are people who waste a great deal of time chasing dreams that are not the ones God has designed for them. The result is frustration and disappointment. We will never go wrong keeping our eyes set on Jesus and doing whatever He leads us to do.

Avoid the trap of blaming someone else. There comes a point when we have to stop pointing our finger at others and saying they are the reason for our insecurities. Parents, teachers, and family members have a powerful impact on our lives, but the greatest influence comes from our personal relationship with the Savior, who always is on our team—pulling for us, believing in us, and cheering for us every single day. At times we will fail, but He will never withhold His love from us. You can leave your insecurity behind because God will never disappoint you when you are living in the center of His will.

Reward yourself when you do the right thing. Many people hesitate about this point. They trust God and gain a victory, but then they stop short of enjoying His goodness by allowing Him to bless them. The author of Hebrews wrote, "Without faith it is impossible to please Him, for he who comes to God must believe that He is and that He is a rewarder of those who seek Him" (Heb. 11:6). If you have successfully reached a goal, then take time to bask in God's goodness and pleasure. Nothing is more rewarding than sensing God's smile and relaxing in His presence.

The major hurdle to overcoming insecurity is overcoming your doubt of God's Word. The apostle Paul wrote,

Who will bring a charge against God's elect? God is the one who justifies; who is the one who condemns? Christ Jesus is He who died, yes,

rather who was raised, who is at the right hand of God, who also inter-
cedes for us.

Who will separate us from the love of Christ? Will tribulation, or
distress, or persecution, or famine, or nakedness, or peril, or sword?
. . . But in all these things we overwhelmingly conquer through Him
who loved us. For I am convinced that neither death, nor life, nor
angels, nor principalities, nor things present, nor things to come, nor
powers, nor height, nor depth, nor any other created thing, will be
able to separate us from the love of God, which is in Christ Jesus our
Lord. (Rom. 8:33–35, 37–39)

Remember, we are more than conquerors. There is nothing too
great for God. Whatever you face in this life, He will bring you through
it. I could have allowed my inadequacies to keep me from living the life
that God designed for me. But I refused to allow Satan to prevent me
from experiencing the joy of having a personal relationship with the
Savior. I feasted on the Word of God and kept reminding myself that
nothing was impossible for Him.

Set your mind on being the person God wants you to be, and see
what happens. I can tell you from experience that nothing will be the
same. The psalmist declared,

> Trust in the LORD and do good;
> Dwell in the land and cultivate faithfulness.
> Delight yourself in the LORD;
> And He will give you the desires of your heart.
> Commit your way to the LORD,
> Trust also in Him, and He will do it.
> He will bring forth your righteousness as the light. (Ps. 37:3–6)

SIX

THE LANDMINE OF COMPROMISE

On the surface, a simple action may go almost unnoticed. It appears to be nothing more than a slight shift in the landscape—an insignificant change that does not matter. However, deep within a person's heart a landmine lays hidden. Something very deadly is under way. It is *compromise*—an attitude that develops and grows stronger with neglect and time. And Satan always seems to find a way to use it to his advantage. He creates his minefield and then tempts us to walk along its surface. First, he gains a foothold in a person's life by tempting him or her to yield to his relentless suggestions: "Just once won't hurt. Don't you get tired of being lonely? Don't you want to be part of the group? This is the way to do it. Just relax, take it easy, and let your heart go free." Satan always has a goal to reach, and it is to draw you away from the Father's love.

Anything that tempts you to abandon what you know is right should be viewed as deadly and dangerous and should be avoided at all costs. Many people fail to do this and become hooked by the subtle and evil lure of compromise, which leads to sin. As children of God, we must learn to guard our hearts and minds against the enemy's deadly traps. Recently an early morning news program spotlighted a certain alcoholic drink. A great deal of time was devoted to the different flavors and even the packaging. An expert talked about how fashionable it was to drink this adult beverage. Soon, several people involved in the interview began to laugh and talk about how they couldn't wait to taste the product after the show ended. This went on for several minutes until their actions became ridiculous and embarrassing.

Satan never reveals the destructive power of sin until after you have taken his bait. This product might have been dressed up in pretty packages, but it contained the same deadly, life-altering drug in every bottle. You may say, "One drink never hurt anyone." Yes, it has, and it still does. It leads to compromise and weakens our commitment to the Lord. One step taken in a wrong direction can do more damage than you will ever know.

THE TRUTH ABOUT COMPROMISE

At some point, each one of us has yielded to compromise. There will be times when we think a single choice will not matter, but it does. Compromise is something that happens deep within the heart and soul of a person. It also increases and becomes more prominent with each step we take away from God's best. Compromise reveals a deeper problem with God's principles and the desire to follow after the very things He wants us to avoid. These include activities, choices, and decisions that He knows will bring heartache to our lives and over time erode our faith.

Like the other struggles listed in this book, compromise will never announce its coming or its deadly intention, which is to destroy your faith and then your relationship with God. If it is left unchecked, destruction is exactly what happens.

Compromise prevents us from doing God's will. We miss His blessing because we turn away from His will and take a path other than the one He intends for us to travel. Over the years, I have heard people say, "God placed me in this position, but things have not turned out the way I thought they would. I just want to be happy. After all, the opportunity for ministry is everywhere. I can serve God loading trucks as easily as I can on the mission field. Plus, I won't have half the pressure that I have now."

The answer to this scenario is "No, you can't." If God has called you to a certain place, you need to stay put until He either moves you or makes it clear that He wants you to leave.

Never forget that there is always a small degree of truth tucked away in every one of Satan's lies. This is how he gets us to compromise our convictions and to do the very things God has told us not to do.

He lures us into his web of deception to trap us and prevent us from being effective for God. It is true: you can serve the Lord almost anywhere and at any time. Yet this does not necessarily mean you are fulfilling His will and purpose. He has a plan for you. You step on a powerful landmine when you decide that you will follow your own plans and not His.

If He has called you to do a certain job, stay at your post until He directs you differently. Even though the situation may be very trying, you will receive a wonderful reward for remaining obedient and not abandoning the work He has given you to do.

If you do leave, you will suffer as a result of your decision. You may experience times of happiness, but the sense of fulfillment will be gone because there is a distinct difference between being in the center of God's will and standing along the sidelines.

Can you make a living doing something other than what you were created to do? Yes, just ask Adam and Eve. God created them to take care of His garden. After they disobeyed Him, all of this changed, and suddenly they found themselves separated from God's blessing (Gen. 3).

The enemy will never caution you to watch your step or to be careful about what you believe. He will never tell you about the deadly power of compromise and its result, which is moral, spiritual, and sometimes physical death. He will taunt you into drifting morally and then applaud your lukewarm decision. It is just one of the ways he seeks to accomplish his work in your life.

Just as the Lord wants you to live to glorify His name, Satan wants to use your disobedience to accomplish his wickedness on earth. When we compromise God's truth, we are about to set off a chain reaction of explosions. We could list many social issues that are up for debate today—abortion and homosexuality are two. Both are dead wrong. However, over time, many believers who are politicians and lawmakers have weakened their stand on these issues. They compromise the principles written in God's Word, and they ignore the fact that the future consequences of their decisions will be devastating for our nation. Satan knows God will not tolerate sin. Therefore, he wants to trick you into believing you will gain something—something you deeply desire—by ignoring God's principles and doing whatever you want to do. Like Adam and Eve, you come up empty-handed.

A COSTLY STEP

I remember a time years ago when my son, Andy, and I were swimming in the waters off the coast of south Florida. We took rafts out into the ocean, but because the undercurrent was particularly bad, we kept drifting away from the place where we had put our towels. I realized if we were not careful, we would soon be far away from where we had started.

I got out of the water and placed a couple of markers on the beach so we would know when we had drifted too far. One marker was quite a distance away from the other one. It did not take long for us to drift past the area I had marked off. I quickly realized that we needed to come into shore or we would find ourselves in a dangerous situation.

Compromise usually involves subtle drifting. You know you are moving, but you don't realize how far away from God you have traveled.

Warning signals may be going off, but the person who compromises his faith will rarely listen. He just floats farther out to sea.

Take David, for example. What began as a seemingly innocent stroll along a rooftop ended in murderous sin. David and Bathsheba's relationship was turbulent due to the compromise and sin that defined their lives (2 Sam. 11).

The enemy always looks for a weak point of entry, and he found it with David. The Bible tells us that when he should have been off fighting battles, he stayed in Jerusalem and ended up compromising what he knew was right before the Lord. He had an affair with Bathsheba and later had her husband placed in harm's way so he would be killed in battle. Their first son became sick and died. Their second son, Solomon, grew up to become king.

After his coronation, David gave Solomon a serious challenge. It served as a warning for the future:

> Keep the charge of the LORD your God, to walk in His ways, to keep His statutes, His commandments, His ordinances, and His testimonies, according to what is written in the Law of Moses, that you may succeed in all that you do and wherever you turn, so that the LORD may carry out His promise which He spoke concerning me, saying, "If your sons are careful of their way, to walk before Me in truth with all their heart and with all their soul, you shall not lack a man on the throne of Israel." (1 Kings 2:3–4)

At first, Solomon was overwhelmed by the magnitude of David's words and the responsibility the Lord had given him. He prayed, "O LORD my God, You have made Your servant king in place of my father David, yet I am but a little child; I do not know how to go out or come in. . . . So give Your servant an understanding heart to judge Your people to discern between good and evil. For who is able to judge this great people of Yours?" (1 Kings 3:7, 9).

Humility marked Solomon's young life. He knew his father's challenge should not be taken lightly. Therefore, Solomon prayed for one thing: wisdom. He committed himself to God and went to work building the temple his father, David, had always wanted to build for the Lord. People came from far and near to seek Solomon's wisdom, which was godly and just.

Later there was a shift in his devotion to the Lord, and he departed from the godly ways of his father. While there was not a quick turn away from God, something happened in Solomon's heart. That something was compromise. Though he continued to worship God, the intensity and desire for His fellowship changed.

On the surface, the shift may have been barely noticeable. However, buried in a list of accomplishments recorded at the end of 1 Kings 10, we read a single entry that reveals when the devastating change took place:

> Now Solomon gathered chariots and horsemen . . . and he stationed them in the chariot cities and with the king in Jerusalem. . . . Also Solomon's import of horses was from Egypt and Kue, and the king's merchants procured them from Kue for a price. A chariot was imported from Egypt for 600 shekels of silver, and a horse for 150; and by the same means they exported them to all the kings of the Hittites and to the kings of the Arameans. (1 Kings 10:26, 28–29)

God had instructed him not to associate with other nations, but Solomon did not do what the Lord required. Life began to go downhill for him.

WHY DO WE COMPROMISE?

What are the reasons we end up compromising what we know is right?

We experience doubt and fear. Doubt clouds our thinking, while thoughts of fear prevent us from moving forward and trusting God.

They tempt us to forget that we belong to Jesus Christ, the Son of the living God and the One who loves us completely and Who has a plan for our lives.

In times of fear, the enemy seeks to draw you off course by using words of doubt: "What if you fail?" "What if the unthinkable happens?" "What if God has forgotten about you?" As a child of God, you have no reason to become fearful or to doubt the truth of His Word. We may not know what is ahead of us, but God does and He is completely in control. The prophet Isaiah wrote,

> Lift up your eyes on high
> And see who has created these stars,
> The One who leads forth their host by number,
> He calls them all by name;
> Because of the greatness of His might and the strength of His power,
> Not one of them is missing.
> Why do you say, O Jacob, and assert, O Israel,
> "My way is hidden from the LORD,
> And the justice due me escapes the notice of my God"?
> Do you not know? Have you not heard?
> The Everlasting God, the LORD, the Creator of the ends of the earth
> Does not become weary or tired.
> His understanding is inscrutable.
> He gives strength to the weary,
> And to him who lacks might He increases power. (Isa. 40:26–29)

Nothing you face will ever be too great for God to handle. There is no need to fear because He never slumbers or sleeps. If He knows every move a sparrow makes, then you can trust that He is completely aware of your needs, problems, and heartfelt longings.

Once you open the door to compromise, the enemy begins to taunt your every step with words that are meant to chill you to the core. He wants you to become fearful and doubt God's ability. Again, his goal is to discourage you and prevent you from living for Jesus Christ. He wants you to become paralyzed with fear, because he knows you won't go forward if you are afraid. You don't have to live in fear another moment. Regardless of what you have done, stop right now and pray for God to forgive you of your sin and to restore the fellowship you once had with Him. If you have never accepted Christ as your Savior, then the first thing you need to do is to come to Him in prayer confessing your need for Him and asking Him to forgive your sin.

Many people feel as though their sin is far too deep for Christ to even care about them. They see it as a stain so deeply engrained that nothing can remove it. God's unconditional love can. He sees our hidden potential and wants us to experience lasting peace and hope. There is only one way to do this, and it is through faith in Jesus Christ. Fear is dispelled when it is exposed to the light of His fellowship and love.

Those who remain steady in their walk with the Lord usually are very sure in their faith. When trouble comes, they know God is right beside them, leading them through the storm. However, a fearful person can be blinded by strong emotions during times of difficulty. Though he knows he should trust God, he struggles with fear and thinks the Lord may abandon him. This is just not true. God will never leave us alone in the heat of the battle. We may have to deal with unusual circumstances, but He will be with us. If you are battling fearful thoughts, ask Him to help you address and correctly deal with any doubts or fears. When you open your heart to Him, He will take you back step by step, if necessary, to the point where you turned away and began to follow after "other gods."

Someone may be thinking, *What I have done is too sinful. God doesn't love me anymore.* There is no sin stronger than the love of God. He has chosen to love us, and He still loves you. Turn in His direction and you will see Him opening His arms to you.

We want to avoid conflict. Rather than express what they know is right, some people will try to avoid a conflict. They may say, "I don't want to hurt anyone's feelings." Or they may say, "If I say something, I'll lose my job." Instead of addressing the shift from truth to compromise, they will cower and allow things to roll along. There are times when we need to speak up, just as there are times when we need to be quiet. If you will seek God's counsel, He will show you what is correct concerning your circumstances.

We have a desire for unity. There are people who do not want to cause "waves." Instead of standing up for what they believe, they hold back and, in doing so, may compromise what God has given them to do. It always is a good thing to seek unity, especially among believers, but it is never good to do this when you end up jeopardizing what you know is right.

We have a deep need for acceptance. If you really need to feel accepted, your convictions will be tested. Acceptance is one of the reasons people do things they know are not a part of God's plan for them. Ask yourself, *Do I want to be accepted by a group of people who could love me today and not tomorrow, or by an eternal, loving, heavenly Father, Who loves me with an everlasting love?* The answer is simple. There is no greater acceptance than God's acceptance. Anything else is many times less than the best. When you make a commitment to be the person He has designed you to be, you will face some challenges. Rest assured, you won't face a single one alone.

We are overwhelmed by peer pressure. Many times, in order to be a part of a group, people will compromise their moral convictions, and the results are devastating. The offices of Christian counselors and psychologists are full today because the guilt of sin is too much for many to bear. You never have to compromise what you know is true and right in order to be a part of a group. There is an eternal sense of contentment that you can enjoy. How do you do this? Recall God's personal love for you. Ask Him to encourage you and help you to make right choices. He wants you to succeed and not fall victim to sin. If someone tells you that he or she will love you more when you compromise what you know is right, walk away. You will never be sorry you did. You do not have to compromise what you know is right. If you are unsure about a situation, ask God to provide the wisdom and discernment you need. He always will. And if there is a question in your mind regarding right or wrong, wait for Him to make His will clear. The enemy will try to tempt you into making a quick, thoughtless decision, but God never will.

We fail to give God what He requires. Many people leave God out of their finances completely. In their minds they draw a line between God and their bank accounts. They go to church and worship God, but never transfer what they have learned through the teaching of His Word to the area of their finances. Whether we admit it or not, God owns everything. He is the One who gives us the "power to make wealth" (Deut. 8:18). When we fail to tithe and to give to His work, we miss a tremendous blessing. We also face the consequences that come from disobeying God. He is specific about giving—it is something we do not want to compromise, especially if we want to obey Him.

We become spiritually weak and discouraged. When we compromise our basic convictions, our very thought patterns become corrupted. After a while, something inside us changes. We begin to view life and our circumstances from the world's perspective and not from God's. Satan's mode of operation is not open attack and then retreat. He never retreats. He hides his landmines in places we cannot see. Even other believers may end up being used by the enemy to create an atmosphere of discouragement and fear around our lives.

This is why the author of Proverbs admonished us to guard our hearts: "Above all else, guard your heart, for it is the wellspring of life" (Prov. 4:23 NIV). The Old Testament viewed the heart as the hub or the center of the emotions and the will. It was considered a starting point for life—all that was held as being true. It determined the course that a person would take.

Today we know that a shift in our thoughts and feelings comes from what we believe, but the principle of guarding our hearts remains true. There is only one way to do this, and it is by hiding the Word of God in our hearts through meditation and worship. The psalmist wrote, "I have hidden your word in my heart that I might not sin against you" (Ps. 119:11 NIV). Spiritual strength comes from one place, and that is the Word of God.

You may feel weak in your devotion to the Lord, but He is your fortress—your deliverer, your shield, and the horn of your salvation—not just in times of trouble but through every season of life (Ps. 18).

We are blinded by pride. Pride is one of the main reasons we yield to compromise. People whose lives are riddled with pride may not even think that they are compromising God's truth. They see themselves as being better and more successful, and as having an entitlement to certain things that others do not. Pride isolates us from God and prevents us from experiencing the depth of His love and goodness. Many times, prideful people fail to realize the extent of their condition until it is too late or until God does something major to gain their attention. The consequences of compromise are prolific. They also are compounded each time we deny God's truth and choose instead to live contrary to His will.

You may think that you can sin in one area but say no to temptation in another. The truth about compromise is this: it begins slowly and spreads. Once you compromise in the way you dress, you will compromise who you date. If you compromise in what you drink or say, then you can count on easing back on your convictions in other areas. I cannot begin to tell you the number of people who have said to me, "If only I had done what I knew was right." "If I had listened to God, if I had sensed His warning then, I would not be where I am today."

For Solomon, compromise began with a single desire: to buy horses in Egypt, but his action led to much more. Once Satan had gained a foothold in Solomon's life, he tempted him to marry women from pagan nations. Soon the king's faith in God was diluted, and he no longer followed the Lord with a singleness of heart.

Here is how compromise works: Solomon reasoned that a small purchase from another country was no big deal. However, the issue soon grew, and he lost his spiritual sensitivity to the Lord. He mistakenly thought marriage to a woman from a pagan culture would not harm him, especially if it created an alliance with an opposing nation. He was dead wrong. Likewise, we are wrong to think we can take any route other than the one God has called us to follow.

THE CONSEQUENCES OF A WRONG DECISION

What happens when you yield your life and heart to the spirit of compromise?

Your character is weakened. Without God, your heart becomes hardened, and you no longer have the foundation of His truth as a basis for your life.

Your personal testimony is diluted and suffers. Often nonbelievers are the first to notice a shift in someone's faith. They notice the compromise and make it clear that they are happy you have broken ranks and betrayed the convictions of your faith.

God's truth becomes irrelevant. Compromise changes the way we view issues such as abortion, homosexuality, adultery, and more. The person who is steeped in sin rarely raises an issue over what is right and what is wrong. Instead, she begins to view sins such as these as social issues that need to be defined by someone other than the church.

You cease to view some actions as being wrong. James understood the struggles of believers. He also knew the depth of sorrow and destruction that compromise brings. He asked,

> What is the source of quarrels and conflicts among you? Is not the source your pleasures that wage war in your members? You lust and do not have; so you commit murder. You are envious and cannot obtain; so you fight and quarrel. You do not have because you do not ask. You ask and do not receive, because you ask with wrong motives, so that you may spend it on your pleasures. You adulteresses, do you not know that friendship with the world is hostility toward God? Therefore whoever wishes to be a friend of the world makes himself an enemy of God. (James 4:1–4)

Compromise was a daily problem for the New Testament church. Most had been devoted to pagan worship before accepting Christ as Savior. They were delivered from a very sinful environment. Like us, they had to guard their hearts and minds with the truth of God's Word to stay pure in their devotion to Him.

People abandon God's Word. The final step to compromise is the abandonment of God's Word and principles. We no longer consider God and what He says about our lives, circumstances, and relationships. This is the most sorrowful position for believers—on our own, away from God, and searching for true meaning.

A COSTLY DECISION

Many times we think that we can slip away and do something that really does not matter that much. How harmful can it be to do something that appears so innocent? After all, do we really need to be legalistic about everything and everyone?

For example, Solomon's actions were not a problem for other nations. However, for Israel, they were a huge problem, because they opened the door to compromise and sin. Only God knows His plans for your life. One thing that is very clear: He calls His people to be holy because He is holy: "For I am the LORD your God . . . be holy, for I am holy" (Lev. 11:44; also see Eph. 1:4; 1 Peter 1:15–16).

If you are involved in an activity and every time you do it or think about it you feel guilty, then you need to know that God's Spirit is warning you that you are standing on a landmine! The spirit of compromise is taunting you to move in its direction. The Holy Spirit shouts, "Stop; don't go there! Don't get involved with it." Unfortunately, we often ignore the warning, yield to sin, and end up detonating the landmine.

Many times when we feel guilty, we are hearing the voice of God. Usually what we hear is the voice of God cautioning us to heed His commands. He warns us when we are out of step with His principles so that we will avoid compromising our Christian faith, witness, and testimony.

You won't lose your salvation when you compromise and do the opposite of what you know is right. Yet you risk losing the very thing that has the ability to keep you steady in times of trouble, and that is your intimate fellowship with the Savior. God will not compete with sin. When compromise and sin are present, He can choose to withhold His guidance and friendship until you confess your wrongdoing.

Solomon was blessed in many ways, but he ignored God's Word. In 1 Kings 11:1–2, we read, "King Solomon loved many foreign women along with the daughter of Pharaoh: Moabite, Ammonite, Edomite,

Sidonian, and Hittite women, from the nations concerning which the LORD had said to the sons of Israel, 'You shall not associate with them, nor shall they associate with you, for they will surely turn your heart away after their gods.'"

Nothing is worth compromising our love and fellowship with God. And we never want to forget that compromise—no matter what face it wears—is evil and destructive.

COMPROMISE DEFINED

Compromise comes when you and I make concessions to believe or act in a certain way. We know that what we have done or said is unwise and sinful. It also can be destructive. This is the kind of compromise we are addressing here.

There is another type of compromise that is useful in business and in situations involving various relationships. We may have an opposing view in some area at work, in our church, or in our neighborhood. Instead of becoming angry and walking away from the situation, we may agree on a compromise in order to get the work done and move forward. It is not sinful. Instead, it is part of our ability to negotiate, cooperate, and work with others.

This was not the type of compromise that touched Solomon's heart. He disobeyed God because he wanted something other than what he already had, and he paid a stiff price for his disobedience. Solomon knew God's commandment. He grew up in David's household and understood the principles of godly living. There were plenty of horses in Israel, but the issue went deeper than material possessions. It struck a cord of sin, which began as an idea of spiritual concession. It was not enough that he had everything a person could desire. Suddenly he wanted his horses to be imported from Egypt—the very place that had once held God's people captive. While he was away from home on a buying trip, the enemy tempted him to become involved with much more than the purchase of a few dozen horses. Once we knowingly start down the road of sin, we have no idea as to the landmines we will face.

We think, *What could be wrong with buying a few horses from another country?* Plenty, if that is what God has told you *not* to do. To be honest, each one of us has done the same thing at some point. We have thought, *This is so small. I really want to do it. Surely God will approve.* But when He has made it clear that we are not to do a certain thing, no amount of pleading and bending of the rules will work. Obedience always involves a choice: God's way or the wrong way.

Lot compromised and ended up in Sodom. Abraham compromised and almost lost his wife. David compromised with Bathsheba and lost a son. Pilate compromised what he knew was true and was denied the opportunity to know the Savior. Compromise is costly.

With this in mind, what are the areas in which we compromise the most?

Morality. We know what is right, but we ignore the truth for fear of not having our needs met. We may also be afraid that if we stand for what we believe, we will face rejection. For example, we know entering a sexual relationship outside marriage is wrong, but often people will excuse what they are doing by saying, "You don't understand the loneliness I feel," or "Things just began to happen and I couldn't say no."

The question is, is it better to say no and remain in God's will or risk the opposite? God does not bless sin, and compromise leads to sin every single time unless we turn away from what we know is not pleasing to Him.

Principles. Often when people are on the verge of compromise, they will ease up on their devotion to God. They say, "I've been busy every Sunday and just have not been able to go to church." Going to church will not assure us a position in God's kingdom. We are saved by faith, but a lack of desire to be in His house usually indicates that something is wrong—out of balance and the first step to failure. It is only through time spent in worship and the study of God's Word that we learn His ways and principles. It is not unusual in today's society to hear someone say, "I know they are living a homosexual lifestyle, but as long as they are not harming me, then I'm not going to say anything about them. Besides, they are nice people."

The fact is that while God loves every sinner, He hates sin. It is open rebellion against Him and His truth, and it does hurt each one of us. Sin, in any form, is the primary element in the erosion of our society. Sadder still is that far too often it is no longer shameful. It is embraced and encouraged by even the church.

Doctrinal beliefs. I remember that a young college student recounted a lecture given by his professor who regarded the Red Sea as being no more than the "Sea of Reeds," a shallow crossing that had become dry and passable by the Israelites. Who would believe this nonsense? The answer is: the same people who fail to believe in the virgin birth and the resurrection of Jesus Christ.

When we compromise our convictions, fail to spend time with the Lord in prayer and the study of His Word, we are bound to end up hedging on our doctrinal views. Too many pastors who stand behind pulpits every Sunday do not believe that the Bible is the inerrant, infallible Word of the living God. They deny its God-breathed inspiration and lead their congregations astray by calling God's sovereignty into question.

Parenting. When you compromise what you know is right, you lose your ability to act wisely. Parents who begin to slip in their devotion to God rarely have the right tools to teach children how to walk wisely. If you are involved in a sinful situation, you will not be able to think clearly about what your children are doing. Beyond this, there is a natural temptation to compromise on certain things, such as what you allow them to watch, listen to, and do.

Some parents may think, *Five minutes won't hurt them*. However, those five minutes could lead to a lifetime of trouble and heartache. A little bit of evil reaps a harvest of sorrow. Remember, when sin is involved, you always reap what you sow, more than you sow, later than you sow. Learn from Solomon who purchased a few horses from Egypt, opening the door to compromise. The powerful alliance he established with this foreign nation later resulted in Israel's captivity. Compromise is serious.

Dress. Over the years, I've watched parents struggle with the way their teenagers dress. There is so much peer pressure on both sides prodding them to conform to whatever society deems right. As believers, we should never do this. There are ways to remain in style and still honor God with our appearance. The goal should always be to ask Him to guide us and not allow the spirit of the world to influence us. I have heard parents sigh, "But I don't want her to dress like her grandmother."

This is Satan's landmine. He wants us to go to an opposite extreme with our reasoning. God always wants us to look our best and do our best. He knows that, without exception, dressing in a provocative manner will lead to compromise.

What we wear and what we allow our children to wear are choices we must make that have tremendous potential for good or evil. The same is true when it comes to the friendships and the habits of our children. If we teach them the value of living for Christ, then when temptations come, they will know how to respond correctly.

Every principle mentioned above also applies to our lives. Honoring God with our lives includes every area. If our goal is ungodly—we want to "catch" the attention of others and motivate them to view us in lustful ways—then we will abandon the very moral principles that God wants built into our lives. Each day we are projecting an image that reflects our inner belief system. If your heart is set on Christ, you will want to be like Him in all that you do, wear, and say.

Music. It is interesting to me that many Christians separate what they do in church on Sunday from what they do during the week. One woman told me that she only wanted to sing hymns when she was in a worship service. A few minutes later she admitted that she never listened to Christian radio but usually listened to something that was far different than anything she sang in the sanctuary.

Living the Christian life requires a lifestyle change that affects every area. If we sing "Holy, Holy, Holy" on Sunday and then hum the words to a song that talks of adultery and sin Monday through Saturday, we are compromising what God has told us to do. "But I love music—all kinds of music," one man told me.

God created all things for us to enjoy; nevertheless, there is a line that He does not want us to cross. Music touches the deepest part of our being. Remember, He created it so that we could worship Him. However, Satan often uses this medium as a means of drawing us away from worship and into compromise.

Most of us know when the lyrics to the songs we hear are not good, but are sensual and written in a way to stir up ungodly feelings and emotions. I'm not against all music. But I would say that if you will think about the lyrics of many of today's songs, you will have to agree that they are not what you would want to listen to in the presence of Christ. Many times we have a tendency to think, *Well, a little bit won't hurt anyone.* Here's the truth: that is exactly what Solomon thought—one horse, one alliance. What could be wrong with that? Plenty when it goes against God's will for your life.

Conversation. The author of Proverbs wrote, "When there are many words, transgression is unavoidable" (Prov. 10:19). He also reminded us, "The words of a whisperer are like dainty morsels, / And they go down into the innermost parts of the body" (Prov. 18:8). Also in chapter 18 we read,

> A fool's lips bring strife,
> And his mouth calls for blows.
> A fool's mouth is his ruin,
> And his lips are the snare of his soul. (vv. 6–7)

James observed,

> The tongue is a small part of the body, and yet it boasts of great things. . . . The tongue is a fire, the very world of iniquity; the tongue is set among our members as that which defiles the entire body, and sets on fire the course of our life, and is set on fire by hell. . . . With it we bless our Lord and Father, and with it we curse men, who have been made in the likeness of God; from the same mouth come both blessing and cursing. My brethren, these things ought not to be this way. (James 3:5–6, 9–10)

Without thinking how it must hurt the heart of God, many people say negative things about others. They also speak lightly about God and dismiss their convictions by listening to a bombardment of words in entertainment settings that they would never want Jesus to hear— words we would not want the Lord to hear us repeat. Many people take God's name in vain or utter profanity with barely a hint of guilt. They compromise what is right and good and wholesome. And their actions dishonor God.

Marriage. Numerous times people have come to me saying how they have fallen in love with a wonderful person. It is always exciting to hear the joy in their voices. But before long, I see a drop in their happy expression. I usually know what they are about to say: "The only problem

I'm facing is she [or he] is not a believer." This is a huge problem that cannot be explained away. The apostle Paul admonished,

> Do not be bound together with unbelievers; for what partnership have righteousness and lawlessness, or what fellowship has light with darkness? Or what harmony has Christ with Belial, or what has a believer in common with an unbeliever? Or what agreement has the temple of God with idols? For we are the temple of the living God. (2 Cor. 6:14–16)

At this point, many people interject that they are witnessing to the person and not planning to marry him or her. They just want to date, but what they are doing is tripping a landmine that they cannot hope to defuse.

Compromise always leads us away from God—a little at first, but the destination is the same—far from God's will. What are you willing to compromise to feel accepted or loved for a short season? This line of thinking may sound very narrow-minded. If it does, then perhaps you have already started down the path of compromise.

These days, a kiss on the cheek is rarely where a couple says good night. If the person you are dating is a nonbeliever, he or she has the ability to pull you down. Over the years, I have seen many marriages— unequally yoked—end in sorrow and defeat. It may be one of the most difficult things you will ever do, but if you know the person you are seeing is not saved, then you need to step away from the relationship until there is an eternal shift in his or her devotion—one that you know without a doubt is sincere.

Money. A significant area of compromise today is that of finances. People are deeply in debt. However, the problem is much deeper than mere debt. It is a matter of submission to God. Paul wrote, "For the love of money is a root of all sorts of evil, and some by longing for it have wandered away from the faith and pierced themselves with many griefs" (1 Tim. 6:10). According to Paul, the problem is not the paper currency we hold in our hands. Our attitude toward money is the problem. Some people have very little while others have a lot. Regardless, if your driving desire is focused on money, then you are caught up in worshiping something other than God, and He says this is sin because it separates you from Him.

God wants to free you from this bondage—bondage that holds you back from being all that He wants you to become. He is the One who has given you the ability to make wealth (Deut. 8:18). Yet far too often, people see their financial situation from a very selfish point of view. They fail to thank God for His many blessings. They also refuse to give back a portion of what He has given to them as a form of worship and adoration through a tithe.

Be aware of this landmine: if you are in debt, you can become defensive and prideful. By doing so you will block God's blessings in your life. We are His stewards, and we will be either wise or unwise. We will be committed or hedge on what we know is right. We should never forget that God has given us so much. If He wanted to take it all away, He certainly could. However, He deals with us in grace, and the least we owe Him in return is complete devotion, praise, and honor.

YOU CAN AVOID SORROW THAT COMES FROM SIN

We can avoid a great deal of disappointment by practicing the principles God has written in His Word. Prevention is always the best route. While we do not need to spend our lives looking for the enemy's traps around every corner, we certainly need to be on guard and not yield to compromising situations.

Most of the time, Satan will hide temptation just below the surface of our lives to lure us into disobedience. He tells us that everyone is seeing the acclaimed Oscar-winning movie. The world loves it. Therefore, it shouldn't matter that it is an R-rated movie. It is funny, bright, and exciting, and we need to do what everyone else is doing. Or the enemy may try to lure us into thinking that if we drink the brightly designed bottles of liquor, we will be a part of a higher social level. But nothing could be farther from the truth.

When we make a decision to do something that damages our relationship with the Savior, compromise has exploded. Feelings of guilt and shame quickly follow. These are just two of the warning signals the Holy Spirit uses to guide us away from sin and back to God. If we ignore them, we will face great difficulty because we always reap what we sow. One step toward sin will lead to another and then another and so on until we are standing at a distance from God. We may become defensive over any suggestion of compromise on our part, but by this point, we are well on our way to sin and failure.

Satan always camouflages compromise. He will bring a sinful thought to mind and then hope that it will resonate within us. Slowly, like a small drip in our emotions, we begin to think about temptation.

Once we notice it and fail to cut it off, the drip becomes steady and consistent. Soon it is a trickle and then a flow that moves throughout our lives—touching our hearts, changing our minds, and altering our commitment to Christ. Compromise whispers, *Just one drink, one look, one wink, one word, one touch, one step.*

I have heard people say, "It felt so right, so different—as though we were the only people who had ever experienced this. For a time, it was wonderful. Then everything began to fall apart." Compromise always ends with disappointment. Defusing this landmine can be difficult, but it can be done with God's help.

Make a commitment to spend time with the Lord in prayer. Whether they are struggling or not, I urge people to begin each day in prayer. This sets a godly tone for your day. It also helps you to be more discerning and able to spot the landmines Satan places along your path.

Even before your feet touch the floor, ask the Lord to guide you through your day. Also, take on the full armor of God as the apostle Paul admonished in Ephesians 6. When you are focused on Christ, you will not be easily tempted to give in to compromise. Paul wrote,

> Be strong in the Lord and in the strength of His might. Put on the full armor of God, so that you will be able to stand firm against the schemes of the devil. For our struggle is not against flesh and blood, but against the rulers, against the powers, against the world forces of this darkness, against the spiritual forces of wickedness in the heavenly places. Therefore, take up the full armor of God, so that you will be able to resist in the evil day, and having done everything, to stand firm. Stand firm therefore. (Eph. 6:10–14)

Time spent in prayer draws us close to the Lord where we worship Him and listen for His instructive voice. It demonstrates our openness to God and our willingness to follow His lead. Prayer is an act of faith. It declares our trust in Him and in His ability to provide the things we need the most. It also reflects our desire to submit our hearts to Christ and allow Him to live His life through us.

Over the years, I have also heard people admit, "I feel so confused. I just don't know what to do next. I've tried to do what is right, but somehow I feel as though I have gotten off track and don't know how to turn my life around." As a believer, you can be assured that confusion is not from God. His way is always clear, sure, and purposeful.

There may be times when He will guide you in a way that does not appear to make sense from a human perspective. Regardless of what you may think, stay on the pathway God has chosen for you to travel since He knows what is best. Do not compromise what you believe is true. He knows what is waiting for you in the future. He may allow you to go through a time of uncertainty because He is going to bless you abundantly. Learning to wait and trust Him for the results is a tremendous lesson.

This is exactly where Adam and Eve made a fatal error. They listened to the enemy's lies, which appealed only to their fleshly desires, and they did not seek God's counsel. The Lord had given them everything they needed to have eternal joy, peace, and prosperity, but they wanted more.

A moment's worth of compromise ended in deep sorrow and regret. If only they had taken time to seek His truth, they would have made a different choice.

We can rejoice in the fact that we do not have to fall victim to sin or compromise. The moment we ask for God's viewpoint concerning our circumstances, He provides this and much more—the strength to stand in times of trial and frustration, especially when we are tempted to leave the God we love.

Read and study God's Word on a regular basis. The one sure way to stave off compromise is to meditate on His truth. Think about it for a moment. How does a football team prepare for the championship game? The players study the playbook—not just for an hour here and there but over and over again until each play is locked into their minds. When they step onto the field, they can run through the plays blindfolded if necessary. They also know the capability of their opponent. It would be foolish to know what you plan to do on third down and not consider that your enemy knows exactly how to execute a passing rush that could ruin your chances at a national title.

Taking time to meditate on and study God's truth positions you for victory. It also prepares you to use the discernment that God provides for every situation.

When a challenge comes, the first few questions you need to ask are: "Lord, how do You want me to respond to this situation? How do You want me to view this? Help me to know Your will or at least be able to accept what I cannot change."

If you are faced with a compromising set of events, you should immediately discern the error and walk away. No matter what the situation, God's Word has an answer. He tells us, "Call to Me and I will answer you, and I will tell you great and mighty things, which you do not know" (Jer. 33:3). If you have a need or desire, God already knows all about it. Studying His Word, asking Him to help you see your life from His perspective, brings fresh insight and often the very hope you need to continue each day. The psalmist wrote, "Your word is a lamp to my feet / And a light to my path" (Ps. 119:105). There are times when you may have only enough light to take the next step. If this is all that God has given you, then take the step and trust Him to give you all you need to see exactly what He wants you to see at this point. He may not want you to see what lies around the next turn. If this is the case, then it is enough.

Once again the psalmist provided insight into conquering compromise: "Your word I have treasured in my heart, / That I may not sin against You" (Ps. 119:11). When you "hide" the Word of God deep inside, temptation comes, but God's truth rises up to meet it and bars its entry.

Ask God to make His will clear to you. If you do not have clear direction from the Lord, do not move ahead. Wait. King David learned to sit before the Lord in worship and prayer. He did not go into the temple to pray and, when nothing happened, hop up and leave. He waited to hear God's word. He may have waited for hours and, in some cases, days until God spoke to his heart. Are you willing to do the same?

It is in times of waiting that you have the opportunity to proclaim your faith in God. Some people do not think they have time to wait for His guidance, but if you rush ahead of Him, you will miss a tremendous blessing. Waiting is not a passive activity. It involves an active faith, and it is necessary if we want to hear God's voice of instruction.

Keep your focus on the Lord. God always has a greater plan in mind for our lives than we can ever achieve on our own. We limit His blessings when we make commitments to things that are not His best for us. If you want to be truly successful, begin by living for Jesus Christ. He is Master of everything. While compromise will seek to draw you away from this line of thinking, the Holy Spirit wants you to exercise your faith in God and know that when you trust Him, He will reward your faith.

Expect God to work on your behalf. When you live according to His principles, He will bless your obedience. He stands ready to reward your desire to follow Him. Just as there are consequences to sin, there are consequences to obedience. These include peace of heart and mind, joy, a sense of purpose, and the abundant love of God.

I often tell my congregation that God always sounds an alarm when we approach sin. However, if we turn a deaf ear, His call to us will grow fainter and fainter until it is almost silent. For example, you may be in a group of people and you feel tempted to repeat some news you heard earlier. God's Spirit cautions you not to say anything, but you ignore His warning. Later you sense a quenching or a sorrow in your spirit. This is the result of your lack of obedience to His Spirit's voice.

There is never a time when you need to disobey God. For whatever reason, He may want you to be still—quiet and resting in Him. Whenever He cautions you to be careful or stop, you need to do it. He is sovereign, and He knows what is best.

Compromise and disobedience shattered the hopes and dreams that Adam had for the future. They changed the course of humanity, but they did not alter God's eternal plan of humanity's redemption. Compromise calls out to us to disregard what we know is true and to do what we "feel" is best without regard to the consequences of our decision. It is a step-by-step process that moves us slowly away from the heart of God. And though it usually begins with a quiet suggestion, it ends with devastation and sorrow.

YOU CAN SAY NO TO COMPROMISE

If you find yourself in a position of compromise, you can do several things to change your circumstances.

First, ask God to rekindle your love for Him. Also pray that He will renew your desire to read His Word and pray. God's Word is your guide to spiritual and emotional healing.

Second, pray that He will help you to restore your faith in Him. Many times, when people have fallen into sin, they mistakenly believe that they need to do something to gain God's approval. There is only one thing they need to do, and that is to confess their sin and need for God. When they do this, God opens their hearts to His love and forgiveness. Faith in God and His ways is the mark of a true believer.

When you place your faith in God, He will lead you out of trouble and heartache. There may be consequences to the sin you have committed, but you will be able to bear them with God's help.

Third, make a commitment to stand firm and listen for God's leading. He is still speaking to us today. He speaks through His Word, pastors and ministers who have made a commitment not to compromise His truth, and godly friends.

As you break your ties with compromise, God will open your heart to His truth, and you will experience an unspeakable sense of joy and freedom. Satan may have blinded Adam and Eve to God's goodness, but the same does not have to be true for you. You can avoid his landmines and live free from the destruction of sin through faith in Christ.

If you have accepted Jesus as your Savior, then your life contains limitless potential because God's Spirit lives within you. Don't allow the world to define who you are or what you will become. Seek God's approval. Surrender your life to Him, and watch as He removes all the things that once held you captive and replaces them with peace, joy, happiness, and a deep, abiding contentment. This is His eternal promise to you.

SEVEN

THE LANDMINE OF UNFORGIVENESS

Someone has hurt you, and you cannot shake the feelings of sorrow that blanket your heart. You get up every morning and tell yourself you need to keep going. But before the afternoon, you are struggling with thoughts of unforgiveness and depression. The days seem empty and the nights are lonely. You tell yourself that nothing will ever be right again. When you have been hurt, how do you handle your emotions?

Disbelief and shock may be your first response. You may even deny the problem exists in hopes that it will go away or get better. You think, *Surely he didn't say that about me.* Or you may respond in anger and frustration, seeking a way to lash out at the other person. "How dare you say that or do that to me!"

A desire to retaliate and to get even can be explosive. In fact, some people feast on this emotion until a root of bitterness begins to grow within them. They are looking for payback, and they won't stop until they have it.

We see this type of scenario played out almost every night on the evening news. Someone hurts another person and tempers flair. Before emotions can be brought under control, anger erupts and someone gets badly hurt.

AN EXPLOSIVE SITUATION

Forgiveness or the refusal to forgive is probably one of the most exhausting struggles we face, because much of the battle takes place in our minds and emotions. We may mentally replay an event that has happened to us and our reactions to it for days or months, and in some cases, years or a lifetime. Some people cannot or choose not to work past the hurts they have suffered. They are stuck in a cul-de-sac of emotion and never take advantage of the opportunity God has given them to avoid the landmines of anger, resentment, bitterness, and fear.

The landmine of unforgiveness is unlike the other landmines. It explodes, but the devastation is not immediate. There is a "click" within your emotions. You feel hurt, disappointed, or angry, but you may deny it by pushing these feelings aside.

As time passes, you reexamine the hurt you have felt. You hold on to it. And slowly the explosive work of unforgiveness takes a toll on your life. As long as you refuse to forgive those who hurt you, you remain bound to them through the anger and resentment you feel. You are not free but bound emotionally and spiritually to this deadly sin.

When we allow unforgiveness to control our lives, we cannot become the people God has created us to be. Likewise, when we refuse to forgive ourselves, we run the risk of suffering deep heartache and depression—the kind that can follow us through a lifetime. And if we fail to accept the forgiveness extended to us by God and others, we can end up suffering the same emotions. We never come to a point where we truly enjoy the goodness and joy of God's blessings.

The Lord created us to live abundantly, but we cannot do this if our thoughts replay past wrongs done to us. The apostle Paul admonished us, "Do not grieve the Holy Spirit of God, by whom you were sealed for the day of redemption. Let all bitterness and wrath and anger and clamor and slander be put away from you, along with all malice. Be kind to one another, tender-hearted, forgiving each other, just as God in Christ also has forgiven you" (Eph. 4:30–32).

HANDLING THE HURTS WE FEEL

Before you can really begin the healing process of forgiveness, you must come to a point where you acknowledge that God is aware of every struggle you encounter. He knows that some of the hurts you have suffered are intensely painful. He understands that you need to grieve, heal, and be restored. However, He is also aware that if you drop your guard and allow bitterness, anger, and resentment to set up shop in your life, you will suffer an even greater emotional pain.

You may think, *There is no way I can forgive the person who has hurt me. The emotional pain and grief are too great.* From God's perspective, forgiveness is a necessary step you choose to take to heal and continue with life. It includes giving up your resentment toward someone else, along with the right to get even, no matter what that person has done.

There are three parts to uncovering the landmine of unforgiveness. Each one is the result of a godly choice.

1. *Choose to let go of every feeling of resentment.* No matter what others have done, forgiveness means not harboring angry feelings against those who have harmed us.

2. *Lay down the right to get even.* I have often heard people say, "I have a right to be mad. You should have heard what he said to me"; or "You don't know what he did. I'm angry and I'm not going to change my mind on this." We must never forget that we do not have rights when it comes to forgiveness and obedience to God. We forgive because He

commands us to do so. This does not mean that what was done to you was okay. God doesn't let the person who harmed you off the hook. You forgive because this is what He desires for you to do.

An unforgiving spirit binds us to the abuser. We may think that in order for the person to be punished, we need to remain angry, but all we are doing is hurting ourselves even more. You extend forgiveness to another person even though he or she may not deserve or ask for this. You are responding like God—like Christ and like the person you were created to be.

On the cross, Jesus prayed for the heavenly Father to forgive the very men who crucified Him. He did not wait for them to say, "I have made a horrible mistake." He knew this was not going to happen. Even in His darkest hour, He was willing to release them, and in doing so, He became the perfect reflection of God's unconditional love for each one of us.

3. *Allow God to deal with the person who has hurt or abused you.* Forgive because this is God's will for your life. Then turn the person over to Him. A common cry I hear is, "If I don't do something, the person who has hurt me will go unpunished." Too many people live their entire lives thinking of ways to hurt or shun those who have hurt them. They are ticking time bombs just waiting for the right moment to go off. Often their anger is not directed at their abuser, but it soon becomes directed to others in their path.

When the brokenness of the past continues to take center stage in your life, you miss God's blessings—one after another. The focus of your life does not need to be on previous hurts. You may need time to heal and deal with problems that deeply touch your emotions. However, you cannot go forward if you are only looking behind.

Forgive and then, if necessary, set up healthy boundaries. You may never see the person who has hurt you again. You must take the important step of releasing your anger, fear, and resentment toward that individual. You can do this in prayer with God, with a trusted Christian professional, or with your pastor.

We may believe we have forgiven others, but we haven't. We continue to think about what they did to us. There is a grinding inside that never stops. Essentially we are not free; we continue to be bound by the unforgiveness we feel.

I do not want to lessen the trauma of some abuse. Yet even in extreme situations, there comes a point where a person must make a decision to live again or remain buried in thoughts of unforgiveness. Many times the person who has caused the trauma we feel may not even know what he or she has done or, worse, care.

One father who had sexually abused his daughter when she was very young never seemed to understand the deep hurt she carried with her each day. Finally she confronted him. His answer to her was far from consoling. His only remark was, "It only happened one time." One time to a child has the potential to linger a lifetime were it not for the emotional healing power of the love of God.

Our world does not have the right tools to repair this type of sorrow and brokenness. Secular counselors may encourage a person to keep going, to look beyond the moment, to pull up his or her bootstraps and not give in to feelings of fear. But only Jesus Christ can reach deep into a person's soul and heal the shattered trust that has been so horrendously damaged. Only God can heal and restore what sin has so deeply damaged.

GOD'S LOVE EXTENDED TO YOU

In the Bible, the woman at the well was a sinner. Her life was steeped in transgression. Over the years she had been married several times, and the man she was with at the time she met Jesus was not her husband.

When a person's life is entangled in sin, brokenness of heart and mind is also involved. We have no idea what went on in the years leading up to the moment she met the Savior. However, we do know that Jesus made a point to stop in Samaria to meet her. He knew her sin, but He also knew the desperation of her heart (John 4:7–38).

God's unconditional forgiveness is summed up in a few words written in a well-known hymn: "Amazing grace! How sweet the sound, that saved a wretch like me! I once was lost, but now am found, was blind, but now I see."

Jesus did not hold any of this woman's sins against her. In fact, He went out of His way to meet her. He was God and He forgave her transgressions. Not only that, He provided the truth she needed to live free of her sin. As they stood beside the well in her hometown, He told her, "Everyone who drinks of this water will thirst again; but whoever drinks of the water that I will give him shall never thirst; but the water that I will give him will become in him a well of water springing up to eternal life" (John 4:13–14).

Have you ever been so thirsty that you longed for a deep drink of cool water? Your soul was parched, and there was a thirst within you that could not be satisfied. Jesus satisfied this woman's deepest longing. She had thought that a person—perhaps the "right" person—was the answer to her restless heart. In a way she was right, but the answer came in the form of God's Son and her desire to worship Him.

Unforgiveness prevents you from worshiping God. It blocks your view of His perfect love—the very love He longs for you to experience. The nature of unforgiveness begins with a simple statement: I refuse to give to others what God has given so freely to me.

Jesus came to the woman at the well just as He comes to you. She accepted His words and on that day opened the gift of salvation. Then she was set free to be everything that God had originally created her to be—a reflection of His forgiveness to others. She got up and headed straight into town where she told the men, "Come, see a man who told me all the things that I have done; this is not the Christ, is it?" (John 4:29).

The Bible tells us, "From that city many of the Samaritans believed in Him because of the word of the woman who testified, 'He told me all the things that I have done'" (v. 39). If she were here, she probably would add these words, "And He was not ashamed to talk with me. He loved me even though my life was filled with sin."

Can you say this? He loves me just the way I am. He has forgiven me and He has plans for my future—ones that include forgiveness, hope, restoration, and love. He is the God of all comfort and the God of eternal love.

FORGIVENESS: DON'T OVERLOOK THIS

Paul instructed us to "be kind to one another, tender-hearted, forgiving each other, just as God in Christ also has forgiven you" (Eph. 4:32). He also reminded us,

> Never pay back evil for evil to anyone. Respect what is right in the sight of all men. If possible, so far as it depends on you, be at peace with all men. Never take your own revenge, beloved, but leave room for the wrath of God, for it is written, "Vengeance is Mine, I will repay," says the Lord.
>
> "But if your enemy is hungry, feed him, and if he is thirsty, give him a drink; for in so doing you will heap burning coals on his head." Do not be overcome by evil, but overcome evil with good. (Rom. 12:17–21)

No one likes to be hurt, but often when we are, God turns our sorrows into blessings. Therefore, no matter what someone has done to you, no matter what has happened in the past, leave the payback to God.

You may say, "There is no way He could use the pain I have suffered—no way good can develop out of this." Yes, there is. First of all, if you handle hurt in the right way, you will turn to Him and not rely on angry emotions to lift you up. Feelings of anger and resentment only tear down what God wants to establish. And He wants you to become a person who forgives and loves others the same way He does. But you cannot do this if you cling to feelings of unforgiveness.

Another thing you need to consider is this: if you have never been hurt, you will not understand the concept of forgiveness. To forgive, you must suffer, and you must also receive forgiveness for any wrong you have committed. Godly forgiveness is an attitude and action that we must learn. It is also rare, pure fuel for the fires of compassion and unconditional love.

He does not want us entering into evil activity, nor does He want us to develop an unforgiving spirit toward anyone. God does not intend for us to live lives of unforgiveness. He wants us to let go of resentment by enveloping our hearts in His love: "Love covers all transgressions" (Prov. 10:12).

Remember what I said earlier: whatever has your attention has you. If you are captivated by God's love, you will live with the light of His love burning in your heart. You will know joy, peace, and contentment. However, if you are angry, bitter, and resentful, you will struggle with feelings of unforgiveness, anxiety, and fear. Your heart will not be at rest, and you will face emotional and physical problems.

God wants you to forgive those who have hurt you so that you will experience the goodness He has for you to enjoy. However, you cannot do this if your attention is locked on how badly you were treated or on the past hurts you have suffered.

You may think, *Nothing has me,* but it does, especially when you fight feelings of hate and anger toward another person. In fact, you have stepped on a horrendous landmine, and at some point, it will explode. So many people wonder why their lives are not going the way they had hoped. The moment we begin to believe that we have a right to be angry is the moment we have switched from following God's lead to setting the pace for our own lives.

A large number of people get off track here. They become focused on the incident that brought pain into their lives. God knows that over a lifetime we will face countless sorrows. Some will come through no fault of our own. In other words, we may be totally innocent and yet end up feeling wronged, hurt, betrayed, forgotten, abandoned, and more.

THE PEACE FORGIVENESS BRINGS

Because of the love of God, we are never alone, never forgotten, never abandoned, never betrayed, and always loved. There is nothing we can do to prevent Him from loving us. Yet a spirit of unforgiveness certainly can distort our view of His intimate and personal care.

One of the most important things you will ever do is to forgive your abuser. My father died when I was quite young. A few years later, my mother married a man who turned out to be very abusive to her and to me. There was a lot of emotional and physical pain in my household as a result of their marriage. At the time, my stepfather never had a positive word to say to me or to her.

I never thought that I would be able to forgive him for what he did to us. However, there came a time when I knew God wanted me to do this very thing—forgive him. I remember asking my mother, "Why did you marry him?" She replied, "I believed you needed a father." She did what she felt was right, and yet it was a very costly decision.

God was determined to bring some good out of this desperate situation. I also realized that it would be very difficult for me to continue in the ministry without dealing with my unforgiveness toward my stepfather.

My mom and I did not deserve to be treated the way we were. No one deserves to be injured or to have his self-esteem destroyed. I knew that if I continued to refuse to do what God was instructing me to do, I would miss a tremendous blessing and risk stepping away from His will.

None of us knows the many ways God will use us if we make ourselves available to Him. This is one reason why we need to be sensitive to the idea of forgiveness. Often before the Lord uses us, He will take us through a time of reflection when He reveals issues within our lives that need to be addressed. Forgiveness may be a part of this process. If so, we need to be willing to forgive the person or persons who have hurt us, but we also need to forgive ourselves. Many emotional problems result from our refusal to forgive.

We talked about compromise in the previous chapter. We need to consider that many times unforgiveness and compromise go hand in hand. If we refuse to forgive those who have hurt us, we take a step toward compromise. God commands us to forgive just as He has forgiven us.

The enemy, however, does not want you to forgive yourself or those who have taken advantage of you. He knows that an unforgiving spirit will lead to feelings of depression, fear, and guilt. With this truth in mind, I made a conscious decision to forgive my stepfather and to move on with life. Did this mean that I would be totally free of every old, hurtful memory? No. But it did mean that I was on my way to emotional healing and recovery. I had taken a sure step toward hope, victory, and peace.

A STEP-BY-STEP PLAN

God has a step-by-step plan concerning forgiveness.

Lift your head and heart toward Him. Seek His shelter and understanding for your circumstances. God knows the pain you are suffering. He knows when someone has done something to hurt you, and one of the greatest promises you can claim is Jeremiah 29:11: "'I know the plans that I have for you,' declares the LORD, 'plans for welfare and not for calamity to give you a future and a hope.'" The prophet recorded these words while the nation of Israel was in captivity.

Jeremiah's personal circumstances were dismal. Most of the prophet's time was spent in a dark, wet, dugout in the ground that may have been called a prison but was more like a grave. From a human perspective, there was little room for hope. However, from God's perspective, hope was definitely on its way.

Often we fail to believe God's promises because we are caught up in thoughts of bitterness and fear. Jeremiah did not do this. He trusted God and found that faith in an unchanging Lord completely altered his outlook. He may be referred to as the "weeping prophet," but he knew that one day Israel's bondage would end. And it did—just as God promised it would.

You may be in a desperate situation, and the last thing you want to do is forgive those who have hurt you. However, if you fail to do this, you will miss the blessing that always follows the storm. Eventually Israel was released and returned to Jerusalem. God restored them, and with their restoration came many blessings.

Pray for the person who has hurt you. At first, this may be difficult, but the quickest way to disarm the landmine of unforgiveness is through prayer. In quiet times alone with God, He will provide the insight and strength you need to understand what has happened. He also will show you how to pray about the situation. If you will fight your battles on your knees, God will move heaven and earth on your behalf.

In the situation concerning my stepfather, I learned that his father had been very hard on him. He had wanted to go to college so he could study to be a medical doctor. Instead, he was forced to stay home and work on the family's farm. He became angry and bitter.

Knowing this helped me to better understand his actions. He was not right. What he did was wrong. However, compassion for him began to grow in my heart because I realized that he did not know how to deal with disappointment. He just became angry and took out his frustration with life on us. Only God has the ability to resolve the hurt we have experienced.

Your situation may not be this serious, or it could be worse. Regardless, the question you must answer is the same one I had to address: How would I allow God to handle my hurt emotions? I knew He did not want me to suffer, but we live in a broken and fallen world. Satan, on the other hand, would love to perpetuate unforgiveness by taunting me with bitter thoughts, resentment, and feelings of guilt.

I chose forgiveness because I could not imagine living with a wall of regret and anger between me and the Lord. I knew this definitely would weaken His ability to use me. As much as possible, God wants us to remain free of Satan's entrapment. He may allow us to experience one difficulty after another. Yet every trial is an opportunity for Him to reveal His faithfulness to us and then to others through the words of our testimony.

YOU WILL EXPERIENCE A SENSE OF JOY AND PEACE

God uses broken people—those who have experienced unspeakable hurts—but it is difficult for Him to use angry, bitter people who think only of how they can receive justice for a wrong done to them.

Once you have forgiven the person who hurt you, you will need to ask God to help you forgive yourself. So many people harbor feelings of guilt for thoughts and actions that happened in the past. Some of this is real guilt, and it needs to be placed on God's altar and left there. Other thoughts and feelings are nothing more than false guilt, which is one of the enemy's favorite weapons to use against us.

Never fall for the enemy's evil accusations. Paul told us, "There is now no condemnation for those who are in Christ Jesus" (Rom. 8:1). God does not condemn us. He forgives us and wants us to do the same for others. Essentially, when we do forgive, we release the other person to the Lord, but we also step out the door of bondage and onto a pathway of freedom that leads straight to the heart of God.

If you want to live free, live for Christ and not for any of the world's demands, especially the demand to hold captive past thoughts of hurts. You have an advocate before God's throne of grace—a mighty Warrior who loves you and will fight your battles for you. James wrote, "Submit therefore to God. Resist the devil and he will flee from you. Draw near to God and He will draw near to you. . . . Humble yourselves in the presence of the Lord, and He will exalt you" (James 4:7–8, 10).

When dealing with forgiveness or the lack of it, a single truth remains consistent: the person who has an unforgiving spirit hurts far more than someone who has grasped the principle of forgiveness and applied it to his or her life.

I've asked people what they do when they sense God's conviction in this area, and some have told me: "I go to bed and try to sleep it off." You can't "sleep off" the effects of unforgiveness, because once it gains a foothold, it quickly builds a stronghold and then buries itself deep within the recesses of a person's life.

You will not understand many things that happen to you—positions you thought you would hold or relationships you were certain would work out.

More than likely as you go through a week, there will be an opportunity for you to feel neglected, overlooked, and ill-treated. Perhaps you feel angry as a result of something that happened on your job, and you want to quit.

What do you do when it seems that you have not been treated fairly? You continue to obey God, and you make a commitment to trust Him regardless of your circumstances. You wait for Him to show you how to respond, and then you act accordingly.

THE BOTTOM LINE TO FORGIVENESS

More than likely, Peter had heard the Lord teach about forgiveness many times. However, he did not understand the principle of forgiveness until after Christ's death and resurrection.

Eternal forgiveness was a cornerstone of Christ's earthly ministry. He came to save us from our sins, but He also forgives us and restores us so we can enjoy God's love and fellowship at every turn in life. You are set free from the bondage of sin and death because Christ died for you. He has forgiven every sin you have committed or ever will commit, and His love demands that you do the same.

Like many of us, however, Peter could not grasp the serious nature of this teaching. He understood the concept of conditional forgiveness but did not see how a person could forgive without obligation or some form of repayment. To forgive for an unlimited number of offenses seemed delusional to him. You and I should be very grateful that Jesus viewed forgiveness differently than Peter did. Without a doubt, we need the forgiveness that has been extended to us each and every day.

When it came to forgiveness, Peter thought he had found a way to act admirably and perhaps even impress Jesus when he asked, "Lord, how often shall my brother sin against me and I forgive him? Up to seven times?" (Matt. 18:21). From a Hebrew perspective, seven is the number of perfection. Peter was sure he had come up with a perfect solution, but Jesus told him to multiply that by seventy. Actually the Lord had an infinite number in mind. God's forgiveness toward us is limitless. And the emphasis of Christ's teaching is the same. He commanded us to extend this same forgiveness to others. Jesus is saying that no matter what the sin or the circumstances, "Forgive those who have harmed you." From God's viewpoint, there is never a time when we should harbor unforgiveness. You forgive just as God has forgiven you.

We are to forgive so that we may enjoy God's goodness without feeling the weight of anger burning deep within our hearts. Forgiveness does not mean we recant the fact that what happened to us was wrong. Instead, we roll our burdens onto the Lord and allow Him to carry them for us.

When I let go of the anger and resentment that I had for my step-father, I was suddenly free to experience God's love and the love of others. I also learned that forgiveness was not that difficult. Once you begin to practice it, you will continue. Then when hurt comes your way, you can address it, but you do not hold on to it and allow it to grow into a destructive force within your life. When you get to the bottom line, there is no way to defend unforgiveness in God's Word.

The author of Hebrews urged us, "Pursue peace with all men, and the sanctification without which no one will see the Lord. See to it that no one comes short of the grace of God; that no root of bitterness springing up causes trouble, and by it many be defiled" (Heb. 12:14–15). To come short of God's grace means that we are unwilling to forgive.

THE FOCUS OF FORGIVENESS

We must stay focused on the love of God, and we must remember that He does not give us what we deserve. Each one of us deserves to be punished for our sins, but Jesus Christ was punished in our place. Whether we like it or not, this also means that He doesn't give others who have harmed us what they deserve. Just as they are responsible for their actions, we are responsible for ours.

Ultimately we suffer the consequences of unforgiveness. There is no doubt that those who have sinned against us will suffer. However, we suffer too when we refuse to do what He commands us to do—forgive and allow Him to deal with those who have hurt us. We may never see His retribution on our behalf. This is not the point. If it becomes the point, then we are setting ourselves up to become bitter, and before we know it, we will drift in our devotion to the Lord.

Darkness and light cannot inhabit the same place. Evil actions such as anger, jealousy, envy, resentment, and unforgiveness cannot remain in the place where God abides through the presence of His Holy Spirit. It won't work, and I am convinced that many of the emotional and physical problems people struggle with today are the direct result of unforgiveness.

Those in the medical profession agree that many of our long-term illnesses come as a result of bitterness, unforgiveness, and emotional stress. Christian counselors and psychologists have long reported that pent-up feelings of hostility, anger, disappointment, and bitterness result in feelings of depression and anxiety along with a host of physical problems. We can stand and watch the downward spiral in the life of a person who refuses to forgive the hurts that have been done to him. He becomes caustic, critical, and suspicious.

You can't hide bitterness. It is going to come out one way or another. Once you develop a critical spirit, people sense it and begin to stay away. No one wants to be with a person who is angry and caustic. When you get to this point, you are no longer in control of your emotions because unforgiveness is controlling you.

You may say, "No, it's not." But it is. It is preventing you from being the person God intended for you to become. You can't think clearly when you are fixated on getting even for what has been done to you. Nor can you function to your best ability when you are hiding in fear over past hurts. The most tragic consequence of unforgiveness is the inability to love.

A bitter person cannot genuinely love anyone else, nor can she receive love. This very fact has a tremendous effect on families as well as other relationships. If you cannot allow yourself to love or be loved for fear of being hurt, then you cut off the most important aspect of the Christian life. God is love. His love for us goes beyond anything we can imagine.

Many people who have suffered deep hurts truly believe that they have opened their hearts to the love of God, but they haven't—not really, not fully, and not completely. They have been hurt so deeply and so many times that even when they do crack open the door to love, they refuse to open it wide and without hesitation.

One woman admitted that in her mind she always reserved a safe place where she could go and close the door to love. In other words, if a relationship did not turn out well, she could quickly close the door to her heart, protecting herself from further hurt and disappointment.

I am not advocating that we leap into friendships and relationships without God's guidance. However, many marriages suffer because one or both spouses do not know how to love one another. Likewise, friendships suffer because love is either withheld or not expressed on a godly level.

We have heard the saying "What our world needs most is love." While this is true, what it needs most is God's love—love that is godly and given without restraint, obligation, or demand. Love so freely given that it motivates us to open our lives, hearts, and wills to love and be loved.

How do you handle the landmine of unforgiveness? You ask God to teach you all there is to know about His personal love for you. Once you get even a glimpse of this, you will want to experience all that you can, and you also will find that you will want to share it with others.

Like the Samaritan woman, you will say, "Come, see a man who told me all the things that I have done" (John 4:29). You will be able to add, "And He loves me unconditionally, even after all I have done."

AT THE ALTAR

There is a place where many Christians end up sinning against God. It is at His altar—the very spot where divine love and forgiveness intermingle as one. Jesus tells us, "If you are presenting your offering at the altar, and there remember that your brother has something against you, leave your offering there before the altar and go; first be reconciled to your brother, and then come and present your offering" (Matt. 5:23–24).

You can learn to deal correctly with an unforgiving spirit.

Deal with anger through godly reconciliation. Most of us know of families that have been emotionally torn apart for years. In many cases, the rift has lasted so long that no one really knows how the problems started or who actually initiated it. Two people who had known one another all the way through college ended up working together at a company in a major city. They enjoyed sharing ideas and debating the best way to achieve their goals at work. They also shared similar interests when away from the office. Then a series of miscommunications jeopardized their friendship. One ended up getting married, and the other accepted a position at a competing firm. They stopped talking to one another and avoided contact; and when asked what had happened, neither could provide a straight answer.

Finally, these two friends made a point of discussing what went wrong. When they realized the separation had taken place as a result of a single thoughtless comment, they were shaken and immediately asked each other to forgive their thoughtless actions.

Some people have not spoken to one another in years simply because of something that was said and never addressed or forgiven. Yet many times those involved go to church every Sunday, sit in the best seats, tithe regularly, and are the first in line to take Communion.

If you have something against another person, you need to know that you are deliberately, willfully holding unforgiveness, bitterness, and resentment in your heart. There is no way you can experience the joy and peace God has for you as long as you remain in this position, because you have a divided mind. James wrote,

> No one can tame the tongue; it is a restless evil and full of deadly poison. With [our tongues] we bless our Lord and Father, and with it we curse men, who have been made in the likeness of God; from the same mouth come both blessing and cursing. My brethren, these things ought not to be this way. Does a fountain send out from the same opening both fresh and bitter water? Can a fig tree, my brethren, produce olives, or a vine produce figs? Nor can salt water produce fresh. (James 3:8–12)

We cannot harbor dark feelings and live a godly, healthy life. We can try to do it, but we are the ones who suffer, and usually the suffering spreads to other areas and to other people we love.

Take forgiveness seriously by admitting that you have a problem. This principle suddenly came to life years ago after I returned home from a two-week vacation. I walked into my study, turned on the light, and could not believe what I saw. Termites had eaten a hole in the wall and were all over the floor. I quickly left and slammed the door behind me. For a few minutes, I felt helpless. What would I do?

The entire time I had been gone and really before I left, termites were eating away at the structure of one wall in my study. Later I thought about how week after week, they had been at work while I was studying God's Word and preparing for the sermons I would preach.

You can deny there is a problem and tell yourself that you are fine, but if you have a spirit of unforgiveness residing within your life, then at some point there will be evidence of the internal destruction taking place in your life. We need to take forgiveness seriously because it is a major issue for every believer.

Assume responsibility for your actions. As long as you blame others for the problem, God will not release you from the guilt you are feeling. Many times, guilt or a strong check in our spirits is His warning sign that something is not right. If we are bitter or angry, we will feel the weight of God's hand over our lives. Some people have difficulty sleeping because God is trying to bring them to a point where they lay down their pride and ask Him to show them what they have done wrong and what He wants them to do.

DEAL WITH THE PROBLEM GOD'S WAY

What do you do when the person who has wronged you is no longer alive? You go to God in prayer, asking Him to heal the emotional wounds you have suffered. Allow Him to show you how to let go of the bitterness and anger you are carrying.

Some counselors suggest writing a letter to the person who has caused your pain without mailing it. Healing takes place when you admit to God that you are hurting and harboring resentment. He does not want you to continue living a life under the threat of enemy attack through feelings of unforgiveness.

Confess what you have done. Be honest with the Lord: "I'm hurting, and I feel left out." "I want to get even with the person who caused such emotional hurt in my life; please help me to see my circumstances from your perspective." When you acknowledge your unforgiving attitude to God, He goes to work to change your view and help you to understand the good that can come from what you have faced.

Lay down your anger. The psalmist told us: "Cast your burden upon the LORD and He will sustain you; / He will never allow the righteous to be shaken" (Ps. 55:22). Just as we choose to be angry, we can choose to forgive. Forgiveness requires surrender, which means that we have to lay our sorrows at the feet of Christ and cast our feelings of anger and frustration on Him as well.

Old-time preachers admonished their congregations to "roll the burden of their hearts over on to the Lord." Today we would be wise to follow this pattern. No matter how heavy the weight of your frustration or sin may seem, God will shoulder it with you when you stop trying to control your circumstances with anger and bitterness.

Make a commitment to pray for the person who is the object of your unforgiveness. You may say, "I don't feel like praying for him. I'm hurt and I'm never going to speak to him again." I understand these feelings.

I did not want to ask my stepfather to forgive me for the resentment I had against him. Nevertheless, that is exactly what God wanted me to do. I had been at my first church for about a year when the Lord began to show me that He wanted me to talk with my stepfather. We never lose when we obey God. He blesses us even when what we are doing is difficult and hard to understand.

The day I forgave my stepfather, I sat down across the dining room table from him, remembering that he was the man who had inflicted so much hurt on my mother. "John," I said, "the reason I came home is to ask you to forgive me for my unforgiving spirit toward you."

He immediately said, "You don't have to ask me to forgive you," but I persisted. "No, I need to hear you tell me that I'm forgiven." He looked up and said, "You are forgiven."

Notice what I did *not* say to him. I did not say, "Forgive me for my attitude toward you when you hurt my mother—when you and I fought over her, when you hurt, despised, and rejected me." There was none of that. If I had brought up a list of hurts from the past, John would have known that I was not sincere.

After I stopped talking, he got up and came around the table and hugged me. He was crying, and he asked me to forgive him for the way he had treated us. He is in heaven now, and I'm glad that I can say that I did not ignore God's call for me to forgive him. Regardless of the past, I forgave him, and God set me free from the bondage of unforgiveness.

You can experience the same release when you trust Him:

- He always works things out.
- He is never caught off guard by the circumstances.
- He uses your sorrows and pain for a greater purpose.
- He has a plan for your future.

Even when we face horrendous trials, we can trust Him to bring good out of the very circumstances that appear dark and foreboding. There is no need to struggle with unforgiveness another day.

If I had refused to forgive my stepfather, more than likely, God would not have given me the opportunity to preach the gospel all over the world. He watches the attitude of our hearts to see if we are fully devoted to trusting Him with every trial and heartache. If I had not been willing to deal with the basic, foundational issue of forgiveness, I would have missed so very much in life.

After this, I remember going to see my stepfather and thinking how grateful I was that the feelings of bitterness and resentment were gone. You may think that unforgiveness will not affect you, but it does. My stepfather was bitter over the way his father had treated him. As a result, he did not have friends. He had difficulty on his job—no one liked him. He lived a miserable life from the time he was a teenager until the day he received Jesus Christ as his personal Savior.

When unforgiveness leads you to animosity, bitterness, resentment, and hostility, you waste your life, and you miss the best that God has for you. You also end up suffering the consequences of your sin. Therefore, don't allow unforgiveness to remain in your life any longer than it takes you to go through the simple steps in this chapter. And never forget: the shortest distance between your sin and God's forgiveness is the distance between your knees and the floor.

EIGHT

THE LANDMINE OF DISAPPOINTMENT

David could remember the feeling of amazement that filled his heart after the prophet Samuel anointed him king over Israel (1 Sam. 16:13). A few years later, though, he had still not assumed his position as king. In fact, from a human perspective, it seemed as though he was even farther away from that goal than when he met Samuel. I am sure there were times when he wondered, *If I am the anointed king, what am I doing hiding out in a cave? Has God forgotten me? Why is He waiting so long to fulfill His promises to me?*

Most of us know the story of how David was forced to leave his home and family in an effort to escape a sure death at the hands of King Saul—a man who was filled with jealousy and envy. Saul knew that one day David would reign over Israel. He became determined not to allow that to take place. God used Saul's unbridled jealousy to force David to wait until he was ready to become king.

DEFINING THE LANDMINE OF DISAPPOINTMENT

Each one of us can remember a time when we have lifted our voices to heaven and asked, "God, why am I having to wait? I'm ready for the relationship, the promotion, the new house, and the next step. I don't want to wait. I know what I'm doing and I want to do it now!"

David, however, prayed,

> Be gracious to me, O God, be gracious to me,
> For my soul takes refuge in You;
> And in the shadow of Your wings I will take refuge
> Until destruction passes by. (Ps. 57:1)

He was learning to live beyond disappointment—something that he would practice years before ascending Israel's throne. There is a strong hint of encouragement in his words, and it is something that each one of us needs in our lives. David knew his survival and his future depended on one thing—God's faithfulness.

In Psalm 139:11–12, he wrote,

> If I say, "Surely the darkness will overwhelm me,
> And the light around me will be night,"
> Even the darkness is not dark to You,
> And the night is as bright as the day.
> Darkness and light are alike to You.

God is not swayed by disappointments. His plans are not deferred or changed as a result of sudden trials or heartaches. He knows our beginning and our end. He is omniscient and all-powerful.

While David did not know the future, he realized that he knew Someone who did. Over the years, there were times when he did become discouraged, but even when pressures became too great for him to handle, David knew the sovereign God of the universe was watching over him. His promises were true, and one day David would become king. Therefore, he avoided stepping on a devastating landmine.

Anything that drives us to the Lord is good for us. Disappointment, heartache, and sorrow are included here. Had God forgotten His promises to David? No, but David was not ready to assume the role of king of Israel. The years he spent battling hardship and disappointment were times of tremendous growth and preparation for the position that he would hold one day.

LEARNING TO RESPOND CORRECTLY

What do you do when feelings of disappointment explode? Do you pick up the phone and call someone as quickly as possible, or do you turn to the Lord in prayer? The psalmist turned to God:

> As the deer pants for the water brooks,
> So my soul pants for You, O God.
> My soul thirsts for God, for the living God . . .
> My tears have been my food day and night,
> While they say to me all day long, "Where is your God?"
> These things I remember and I pour out my soul within me.
> For I used to go along with the throng and lead them in procession
>   to the house of God,
> With the voice of joy and thanksgiving, a multitude keeping festival.
> Why are you in despair, O my soul?
> And why have you become disturbed within me? (Ps. 42:1–5)

Each one of us will go through times when we feel discouraged and disheartened. Many people want to quit, give up, and walk away, but as believers, we should never give in to these feelings.

People who have never accepted Christ as their Savior do not have the living hope that Christians have. Over the years, I have even seen believers become so discouraged that they want to turn and walk away from what God has given them. When they do, they detonate a landmine.

My caution to everyone reading these words is very simple: when disappointment strikes, don't give up and don't give in to thoughts of discouragement. You never know what God has waiting for you. Like David, you may go through a long season of waiting when disappointment seems to follow your every step. However, each series of trials prepared David for some aspect of the job that he would have one day.

Even if you are older and the enemy has tempted you into believing that your life is almost over, don't believe it. God uses people, and there is never a time limit on what He can do in and through us. Therefore, when problems come, turn to Him in prayer. Make sure that He is the first one who hears your cry for help and understanding. While we need the support of godly friends, we need God's comfort and wisdom first, or we risk being overwhelmed by sorrow when it comes, especially if it lingers as it did in David's life.

I remember when a situation that I was facing seemed so dark and discouraging that I did not know what I would do. I would wake up at night and think, *God, what will happen next?* Then I would get up and lie down on the floor next to my bed and pray. Many times, I would ask the Lord to encourage my heart, change my attitude about my circumstances, and help me to lay the burden that I was carrying at His feet. I would also ask Him to help me get back to sleep. He never failed to do this.

I am sure there were times when I tossed and turned, but I learned a very important lesson. If I stayed focused on God, I would have the help, strength, and ability to keep going, even though it felt as if my world was crumbling around me. In the middle of a very dark time in David's life, he wrote, "Even though I walk through the valley of the shadow of death, / I fear no evil, for You are with me" (Ps. 23:4).

God is omniscient, omnipresent, and omnipotent. We can rest in His presence because we know that He has only the best for our lives and He will not allow the enemy to harm us. If disappointment, sorrow, or trouble comes, He will teach us how to respond and lead us to a place of blessing and hope.

You are never alone. The enemy may want you to think you are, but you are not. Even before His death, the Lord told His disciples that He would return to them (John 14:1–3). Often the very thing we need to hear in times of trouble is Christ speaking these words to our hearts, "I will not leave you as orphans; I will come to you" (John 14:18). We also need to remember that God never begins to work in our lives only to abandon His plan. Once He begins, He will continue until it is completed (Phil. 1:6).

You may feel as though your life is a mess. From a human perspective, it may seem this way, but never forget that God—who is infinite in knowledge—can take the most troublesome circumstances and turn them around for good. The question to ask whenever trials come is this: "Lord, what do You want me to learn in this difficulty? How can I become more like You by suffering this pain, traveling this road, and submitting to this heartache?"

God knows what suffering feels like. He watched as His Son died a painful death on the cross for something He did not do. He heard every breath, every cry, and every whisper Jesus made on that day. He also knows the depth of your disappointments. But just as He had a greater plan for Christ's life, He also has one for you. If you never face disappointment, you will never know how to trust God, encourage others, or live in the comfort of His care.

Disappointment is an emotional response to some failed expectation or some desire that we have. It comes when we lose our godly motivation and drive, which bring fulfillment and purpose to life. When we lose these, our hearts can become heavy and sad.

While disappointments are a normal part of life, they can tear a gaping emotional hole in our hearts and emotions. There will be times when we are ignorant of the storm clouds that are gathering. We may experience a series of disappointments, and suddenly we feel over-whelmed by our situation and long for encouragement.

Remember, the psalmist wrote, "As the deer pants for the water brooks, / So my soul pants for You, O God" (Ps. 42:1). He was longing for the Lord; in verse 5 he admitted his struggle with feelings of despair along with his deep need for God's help.

We can ignore the problem and, in a strange way, end up feasting on the attention we receive as a result of our discouraging circum-stances. I would not recommend following this plan of action. One of Satan's primary goals is to discourage you. He wants you to quit, throw in the towel, and walk away from the work or the plan that God has given you. In fact, you may not be in a high-profile job.

This does not matter to the devil, especially when his desire is to destroy you through the landmines he places in your path. If he can depress you and create anxiety within you, he will do it because he believes he will be on his way to gaining a stronghold in your life. And he is right. There is never a time when it is okay to ignore the problems we are facing or to allow them to grow to a point where we can no longer think clearly about God's goodness and faithfulness.

Each one of us knows someone who is hurting, and yet, in between the words of sorrow and grief, we also hear snide, bitter comments. This is a dangerous place to be because if we do not deal promptly with disappointment, it can turn into discouragement and then into depression.

Adversity is a weapon that the enemy will try to use against you. However, you do not have to allow him to gain access to your thoughts or your life through disappointment. While this is a weapon in the hand of the enemy, it is a tremendous tool in God's hand.

You may not understand why your employer said no to your request, why you were passed over for a promotion, or how you will ever reach some of the goals you have set for yourself. God knows, and this is all that counts. He can change the circumstances of your life more quickly than you can imagine. But if you become mired in anger and frustration as the result of disappointment, you may never experience all the good He has for you.

IDENTIFY THE SOURCE OF DISCOURAGEMENT

One way we move past the landmine of disappointment is to identify its type and source. Without a doubt, Satan is the number one culprit. His existence is devoted to seeking ways to damage our testimony and prevent us from fulfilling God's will.

He wants you to focus only on the negative aspects of your situation. Therefore, he will taunt you with words of discouragement: "You will never reach your goals." "Your life will never amount to anything worthwhile." "You're not smart or good looking." "No one loves you." "No one values you; if they did they would include you in their plans." "You just need to give up." Satan rattles off one lie after another.

Many times, his voice hits a nerve because some people grew up in homes where these same messages were drilled into their heads. After a while, the messages are imprinted in their minds. Then when disappointment comes, the first thing that comes to mind is: "It must really be true. My life is a mess just like Dad said it was."

A negative, critical spirit will destroy a child's hope for the future. It will break his spirit and leave him floundering in doubt unless he reaches a point where he can tap into God's truth concerning his life. Don't give in to negative thoughts, and don't allow yourself to be the one who passes wrong attitudes on to others just because you experienced disappointment. God still has a plan for you.

Other causes of disappointment include situations that we may not consider at first. For example,

- *areas of weakness.* These can include gossip, lack of forgiveness, anger, feelings of bitterness, or lustful desires.

- *unrealistic goals for our lives.* We need to set healthy goals for our lives. This means being realistic but not negative. Some people cannot imagine God blessing them in their vocations or personal lives. However, He does and He will. We need to set goals that will encourage us to trust Him with every area of our lives. If we set goals that are too grand, we may find ourselves struggling with disappointment and a sense of failure.

There are many consequences of disappointment. The one that tops the list is *prayerlessness.* Once disappointment drifts into discouragement, the person usually stops praying. He becomes critical, cynical, and angry with God. He is likely to say something along these lines: "He is God, right. I mean, He could have stopped it."

Nothing blocks prayer the way anger does. If you have become disappointed with God, you need to force yourself to go to Him in prayer. Get down on your face, and ask Him to forgive you for doubting and not believing that He is in control of all things.

Mary and Martha did not understand why Jesus did not come when they first sent word to Him that their brother was dying. He was their friend. His lack of response did not make sense. However, Jesus had a far greater plan in mind. He raised their brother from the grave. Though disappointment may hurt emotionally, God always is at work to bring fresh hope to our lives.

Another consequence of disappointment is *a divided mind.* We cannot think clearly when we focus on Satan's lies and negative words. One man spent his entire life living in fear and disappointment because he viewed himself as a failure. His mind was divided, and he could not focus on the truth of God's Word. If he had, he would have quickly learned that all things are possible when we believe in God's Son.

Often when we face disappointment, we want to *blame* someone for our problems, or we blame God. There are times when no one is at fault. Problems come because they are a part of life. But your response to them is what is important.

We also become *angry,* and if this is not taken care of quickly, we will become *depressed* and *self-centered.* The definition for depression is simply anger turned inward. When we hold destructive anger inside and do not release it to God, we will suffer depression, anxiety, and a host of physical problems. God did not create us to live and abide with frustration, anger, and resentment. He created us to experience His joy and goodness. If our minds are set on our problems, we will never know the many blessings that God has for us.

Disappointment leads to isolation. We pull away from others and sulk in our misery. Rather than rejoicing over God's forgiveness of the people of Nineveh, Jonah ended up depressed, sitting under a broom tree (Jon. 4). He was angry and frustrated with the Lord because the situation had not turned out the way he wanted. The Ninevites were Israel's dire enemies. Yet God had commanded him to go and preach repentance to them. Jonah wanted to see this wicked nation destroyed, but God wanted to save it. Therefore, He extended His mercy to those living in this region.

Like Jonah, we can become critical, demanding, and demeaning of others. We notice that those around us are happy and getting ahead, and instead of joining in on the fun, we distance ourselves from friends, coworkers, and family members.

STEPS TO MOVING BEYOND DISAPPOINTMENT

At first a young man who lost his job thought he would never get over the disappointment. He was not prepared for the feelings of loss after he was told to clean out his desk. However, a week later, he was able to think through the circumstances that led to the moment when he was laid off. He had been working ten to twelve hours a day—sometimes six to seven days a week. He had only been married a short time, and his relationship with his wife had become strained.

The layoff from work provided the right opportunity for him to stop and ask God to help him gain the right perspective for the future. Sometimes God allows disappointment to correct our position. Regardless, the goal of any disappointment is the same: to sharpen our focus on God and to prepare us for a greater blessing. To view it differently is to dismiss the faith God calls us to maintain.

How do you handle feelings of disappointment and discouragement?

Realize that God is aware of your circumstances. Nothing catches Him off guard. He knew that adversity would strike you. Therefore, let your first reaction be one that is turned in His direction: "Lord, help me make sense of all of this. I'm hurting and I don't understand what is going on. I know You are aware of my situation and how my heart is breaking. Please show me the way through this time of disappointment."

I have seen older people who worked many years at a company go through a layoff or a demotion. Usually one of the first things they ask is, "What will happen to me? How will I face another day?" In times of adversity, you must remember that while you may be utterly stunned by disappointment, God never is.

We live in a fallen world where decisions are often made without deep thought as to how our lives will be affected. This is where the mercy and grace of God come into play. If you will trust Him during a difficult season, you will find that He will help you move past the hurt to a place of extreme blessing.

Understand that disappointment is a part of life. As much as you would like to isolate yourself from pain of any kind, you can't. Disappointments will come. You will have to make a choice about whether to become angry and overwhelmed by the situation or to allow God to work in your circumstances.

While you need to acknowledge the feelings that have welled up within you, you also need to stand firm in your faith. Has God ever failed you? He never has. He may have allowed some things to turn out differently from the way that you planned or even desired. But every single time you faced a moment of discouragement, He was right beside you, longing for you to ask for His strength, wisdom, and insight.

Many times, people do not do this because they want to feel a little depressed so they will gain extra attention. In other words, they enjoy self-pity. There is a problem here that often goes unnoticed until it is almost too late. Satan is plotting and planning your discouragement.

God does not want us to suffer. However, there are times when He allows disappointment to touch our lives for a greater purpose. He draws us closer to Himself. James wrote, "Draw near to God and He will draw near to you" (James 4:8). If you resist Him, the burden of your heart will only grow larger and heavier.

The people who received James's letter were not living lives of ease, comfort, and pleasure. Most were part of what is known as the Dispersion or, in the Greek language, the *Diaspora*. Many Jewish believers had been forced by the Roman government to leave their homes and families. Some left voluntarily and others under the threat of Nero's wickedness and violence against Christians. The point James is making is that regardless of your circumstance, you can have an eternal sense of joy and peace deep within your heart.

He also challenged them to "consider it all joy, my brethren, when you encounter various trials, knowing that the testing of your faith produces endurance. And let endurance have its perfect result, so that you may be perfect and complete, lacking in nothing" (James 1:2–4).

God's joy is not based on anything this world has to offer. It is rooted in the eternal promise that you have been given through Jesus Christ. That is, if you will place your faith in Him, He will save you from your sins and an eternal death. He also will give you the grace to reside with hope regardless of your circumstances. These Jewish believers needed to be reminded of the ways of God:

He is faithful.

He loves you with an everlasting love.

He is near to everyone who believes in Him.

He will provide a way through every difficulty.

He is your burden bearer.

Be hopeful because hope is contagious. Think for a moment of all the people you know who are suffering some form of disappointment. Like most of us, you can probably name several. On a broader scale, we know there is tremendous suffering and discouragement in our world. When we encourage someone else who is hurting, we receive a blessing as well.

First of all, we need to remember that God has never failed to keep a single one of His promises. There is hope for even the darkest situation because Jesus is our eternal light. Therefore, when we learn to offer hope to others who are hurting, we are doing what He has done for us. We are offering hope that does not bring disappointment (Rom. 5:5). The fact is, hope and disappointment cannot coexist.

The psalmist asked,

Why are you in despair, O my soul?

And why have you become disturbed within me?

Hope in God, for I shall yet praise Him,

The help of my countenance and my God. (Ps. 42:11)

Second, just as hope is contagious, disappointment can breed the same in those around you. Discouragement, cynicism, and anger can affect friends, family members, and coworkers.

Most of us have experienced this at one time or another. We pick up the telephone and call a friend or a family member only to find ourselves wondering why we made the call. After a few minutes of hearing all that is going wrong in his or her life, we suddenly feel discouraged about our own situation.

When this happens, it is good to remember that disappointment only lasts a season. If you are facing a serious illness, you may feel as though it is lasting a lifetime. I have seen believers who have had cancer and remained steadfast in their faith. On the other hand, I have watched in sorrow as others have sunk into depression and longed to leave this life.

The apostle Paul reminded us, "No temptation has overtaken you but such as is common to man; and God is faithful, who will not allow you to be tempted beyond what you are able, but with the temptation will provide the way of escape also, so that you will be able to endure it" (1 Cor. 10:13). In this setting, Paul used the word *temptation* to speak of suffering, disappointment, and trial.

The Greek word *peirasmos* means trials with a beneficial purpose and effect. They are allowed by God but only with the expressed purpose of spiritual refinement whereby you become more like His Son. God's goal is always to draw you close to Him. He wants to shape your life so that you reflect His love, mercy, grace, and faithfulness to others.

Once you learn the reasons for disappointment, you will also understand there is a correct way and a wrong way to respond to the trials of life. The wrong way is to become critical, cynical, and depressed. These are the evidence of Satan's handiwork, and they do not belong in the life of a believer.

Recognize that disappointments can be conquered. When adversity comes, you have a choice to make. You may say, "Now, wait a minute. I didn't choose to become depressed. It chose me!" How disappointment came into your life is not the issue, but your response to it is. You may be shocked, hurt, and angry, and you may want to run. That's okay. Yet if you cling to any one of these, they will bind you away from God's goodness, and your circumstances will become more dismal.

The author of Hebrews encouraged us not to give up: "All discipline for the moment seems not to be joyful, but sorrowful; yet to those who have been trained by it, afterwards it yields the peaceful fruit of righteousness" (Heb. 12:11). We are disciplined or trained by disappointment to trust God with an undivided mind and heart. We conquer disappointment by standing strong in our faith and not wavering through doubt or self-pity.

Paul lifted our confidence with this reminder:

> Who will separate us from the love of Christ? Will tribulation, or distress, or persecution, or famine, or nakedness, or peril, or sword? . . . But in all these things we overwhelmingly conquer through Him who loved us. For I am convinced that neither death, nor life, nor angels, nor principalities, nor things present, nor things to come, nor powers, nor height, nor depth, nor any other created thing, will be able to separate us from the love of God, which is in Christ Jesus our Lord. (Rom. 8:35, 37–39)

Many times we are tempted to think, *Well, that is Paul talking. Surely he did not face the trials and temptations that we face today.* The fact is, in most cases, he endured situations that were far more severe than what we encounter today. He told us about them in 2 Corinthians 11:24–28:

> Five times I received from the Jews thirty-nine lashes. Three times I was beaten with rods, once I was stoned, three times I was shipwrecked, a night and a day I have spent in the deep. I have been on frequent journeys, in dangers from rivers, dangers from robbers, dangers from my countrymen, dangers from the Gentiles, dangers in the city, dangers in the wilderness, dangers on the sea, dangers among false brethren; I have been in labor and hardship, through many sleepless nights, in hunger and thirst, often without food, in cold and exposure. Apart from such external things, there is the daily pressure on me of concern for all the churches.

Paul had one opportunity after another to become discouraged, but he never did. Instead, he wrote in Philippians 4:13, "I can do all things through Him who strengthens me."

When disappointments come, what do you do? Do you ask God to give you His perspective? Or do you think, *Life is so bad. I can never get ahead*? Or do you pray, "Lord, this is certainly difficult. Please show me how to respond to the trial that I am facing. Help me to learn what You want me to learn through this difficulty"? An open heart to God is a foundational step to gain strength and freedom during deep disappointments.

GOD HAS A WONDERFUL PLAN

When a person's life has been blown apart by disappointment, he will not be able to think clearly or with God's principles in mind. Instead of working through an issue with the Lord in prayer, he may react to the problem by saying things he wishes he could take back later. Or he may make an unwise choice that only brings more disappointment.

When we feel let down by God, we need to deal with our feelings immediately. Far too many people drift in their devotion to God as a result of harboring discouragement in their hearts. There was a time when they went to church, studied their Bibles, and worshiped the Lord through praise, song, and prayer, but not anymore. They have become disappointed with life and with Him.

Disappointment can be a breeding ground for bitterness and resentment. These can literally eat an emotional hole in your soul if you are not diligent with your thoughts and devotion to God. One woman who was struggling with depression commented, "I just don't feel like getting up and going to church anymore." Church, however, was the very place she needed to be. If you are struggling in any area, the smartest thing you can do is to ask God to lead you to a Bible-believing church where you can hear His Word taught without compromise.

The world cannot encourage you. It will only lead you farther into cynicism and despair. Satan is the prince of this world, but you do not want to fall under his influence. No matter what it takes, get into God's Word and ask Him to guide you through the darkness you are facing. When you do, He will answer your prayer and also bring a light of hope to your situation.

How do you emerge from disappointment? You probably have read Psalm 23 many times. However, I want you to see several important principles written within this psalm.

First, realize David wrote these words during a very trying time. He was in an emotional valley, but he also was facing an extreme physical threat. When disappointment comes, the first thing we need to do is exactly what David did. He turned to God. The evidence is his leading line into the psalm: "The LORD is my shepherd, / I shall not want" (v. 1).

Within these few words, we gain a concise picture of David's unshakable faith in God. When trouble comes, many people immediately ask, "What am I going to do?" They look within themselves for the answer, but David knew who was the source of his strength. God would show him how to deal not only with the situation but also with any feelings of disappointment.

He went on to write, "He makes me lie down in green pastures; / He leads me beside quiet waters" (v. 2). When our hearts are in tune with the Lord, we will have a quiet, restful sense of peace. Even though we may be in the middle of very trying times, we will be able to do what David did—walk straight through the valley without becoming overwhelmed by fear.

Peace is the natural overflow of a heart that is set on Christ. You may or may not know why God has allowed you to encounter disappointment, frustration, or deep sorrow. Regardless, the one thing that matters the most is the focus of your faith. Is it set on God or on your ability?

David's heart was set on God. Therefore, he could write,

He restores my soul;

He guides me in the paths of righteousness

For His name's sake.

Even though I walk through the valley of the shadow of death,

I fear no evil, for You are with me;

Your rod and Your staff, they comfort me. (vv. 3–4)

If you truly want to have peace in your life, trust God with your problems, your future, and your very life. He has only good plans for you, but you must be willing to walk with Him through valley times as well as times of carefree joy.

Second, David admitted that there was a problem. He did not try to deny it or ignore it. Whatever he was facing, it felt dark and stressful. Remember, he was the anointed king of Israel, but God had not placed him on the throne as yet. He lived each day with a promise from God tucked deep down in his heart.

We have to wonder how many times Satan whispered, "You are never going to be king," or "You will die in battle before you take the throne." The enemy's existence is based on his ability to draw us away from God through doubt. However, David did not doubt. He had a personal, loving relationship with the God of the universe, and he knew that at the right time, every promise that the Lord had given him would come to pass.

David took this a step farther; even if nothing came to pass, he would continue to trust in the Lord his God. He had learned a key principle: "Without faith it is impossible to please [God], for he who comes to God must believe that He is and that He is a rewarder of those who seek Him" (Heb. 11:6; also vv. 32–33).

Third, David understood that God did not send the trial he was facing. The Lord had allowed it for a purpose. Instead of sinking deep into despair,

David responded along the lines that he had been taught to follow: he immediately turned to God, he admitted there was a problem—a trial—and he did not have the ability to face it on his own. Then he refused to become overwhelmed by the enemy's attack. He was discerning enough to realize that God had something He wanted David to learn.

The same is true for you. When trouble comes, you can know without a doubt that there is something within the trial that God wants to teach you. The question is, do you want to learn it? David wanted to learn even more about God and His ways, and I trust this is your goal as well.

Fourth, David did not shift his focus; it remained on God. There will be times when you receive conflicting information. One person tells you one thing, but your mind pushes you in another direction. If there is a battle going on inside you, ask God to make His way and will perfectly clear to you.

The wisest thing you can do is to get on your knees with the Word of God and cry out, "Oh, God, speak to my heart. Show me what I need to do. Help me to hear Your voice so I will have clear guidance through this distressful time."

Sometimes when you do this God will catapult you right out of discouragement because you have turned to Him in faith. You trust Him, and there is no way He will overlook your prayers (Jer. 33:3).

David often recalled the times God had delivered him in the past. The cornerstone of his faith was God's faithfulness. Time after time, he had witnessed God's goodness at work in his life. Therefore, he could say, "You prepare a table before me in the presence of my enemies; / You have anointed my head with oil; / My cup overflows" (Ps. 23:5).

Finally, David confessed with his mouth that God would do exactly what He had promised. He was God, and there was none beside Him. God was in complete control of David's life: "Surely goodness and lovingkindness will follow me all the days of my life, / And I will dwell in the house of the LORD forever" (Ps. 23:6). When it came to devotion, there was no question in David's life. He was totally committed to God.

You can defuse the landmine of disappointment by confessing the truth of God. Turn to His Word, and study about His faithfulness, attributes, and personal promises to you. Dig deep and you will gain an awesome perspective of His nature—who He is and the depth of His intimate love for you. He always listens when you pray to Him, and He will come to your aid, just as He did for David.

NINE

THE LANDMINE OF FEAR

With London's bombed-out buildings in the backdrop of his mind, Winston Churchill stirred the wavering faith of his nation with these words: "Never give in, never give in, never, never, never, never—in nothing, great or small, large or petty—never give in except to convictions of honour and good sense. Never yield to force; never yield to the apparently overwhelming might of the enemy."

England was on the brink of disaster. The people had endured months of daily air raids and bombings. Many of the city's children had been sent to live with families in the countryside—strangers willing to take them in and protect them. Fear filled the hearts of the people and would have overcome them except for two things: their will and their faith.

In 1942, Churchill said, "Now, this is not the end. It is not even the beginning of the end." The British people along with their allies went on to win the Second World War, but not without serious loss and intense suffering. At any point, they could have caved in to fear and given up the freedom that was so precious to them.

A PERCEIVED THREAT

The landmine of fear is a powerful weapon. Like the other landmines mentioned in this book, it has the ability to prevent us from experiencing the blessings of God. However, the landmine of fear takes this concept to an entirely deeper level. It can paralyze us to such a degree that we lose our godly perspective concerning our circumstances. It clouds our vision for the future and leaves us struggling with doubt. When our lives are shrouded in fear, we cannot imagine the goodness that God has for us.

The British people faced a very real threat. Yet even though they endured night after night of attacks for many months, the light of their hope did not go out. In fact, a remarkable thing began to occur. The more they were bombed, the more they became determined not to give in to the enemy.

There are times in our own lives when the battle with fear seems to grow to a point where we feel tempted to give up. What may have started as a subtle threat quickly escalates to a point of serious warfare. Like the British people, we have a choice: we can succumb to fear or we can use it to strengthen us in our walk with Christ. How is this done? Whenever you place your faith in Christ and become determined not to fall victim to the landmine of fear or any other landmine, you find that God gives you strength for the battle. The prophet Isaiah wrote,

> [God] gives strength to the weary,
> And to him who lacks might He increases power. . . .
> Those who wait for the LORD
> Will gain new strength;
> They will mount up with wings like eagles,
> They will run and not get tired,
> They will walk and not become weary. (Isaiah 40:29–31)

What is your greatest fear? Someone reading these words may not even know. Inside there is a tension—a residing fear—but there is no way to define it. It is there most of the time, and you wonder whether you will ever be free of its grasp. The answer is yes! Freedom will come; however, first you must believe that God has the ability to deliver you.

You must come to a point where you know that God is who He says He is and that your future and all that concerns you are wrapped up in His loving care. There can be no doubt. When you know this, even when the storms of life strike, you will not be driven off course.

If England had given in to the enemy, the world would have a much different look today. The same is true for us. If we yield to Satan's words of anxiety and fear, our lives change dramatically. They take on a different appearance and become something other than what God wants us to experience.

A fearful person wonders what difficulty or trying situation is waiting for him around the next turn in the road. He worries that something will go wrong, and it will be beyond his ability to handle it. He does not realize that by buying into fear, he has stepped on one of the most destructive devices there is—the landmine of fear.

While some trials may seem more than we can handle, they are never more than what God can handle. The apostle Paul reminded us, "Faith comes from hearing, and hearing by the word of Christ" (Rom. 10:17). We must never forget that the first step toward conquering fear is gaining truth and knowledge. When thoughts of fear occur, we must make a choice based on the truth we know. If our minds have been programmed with the Word of God, we will be able to discern truth from fiction—a real threat from a perceived danger.

Some people hear God's Word taught in church, but they never apply His principles to their lives. Therefore, when a threat comes, they feel defenseless. But they are not. Jesus told His followers, "Are not two sparrows sold for a cent? And yet not one of them will fall to the ground apart from your Father. But the very hairs of your head are all numbered. So do not fear; you are more valuable than many spar-rows" (Matt. 10:29–31).

There will be times when we wonder whether God really understands what we are facing. We can be sure that He does. He never leaves us, and He always provides the strength and wisdom we need for every situation.

The enemy is watching too. He is ready to launch a fearful attack against your heart, but you do not have to become his victim. You have a mighty arsenal at your disposal through Jesus Christ.

In the book of Nehemiah in the Old Testament, we read how the walls surrounding the city of Jerusalem had been torn down through enemy attack. Most of the people had left or were taken away into cap-tivity. There appeared to be no hope for rebuilding the walls. Yet God stirred Nehemiah's heart to do the work.

In those days, a wall around a city meant protection and security. Without fortified walls, residents were vulnerable to enemy attack. While Nehemiah went to work on the reconstruction of the walls, his enemies also went to work.

They issued one fearful threat after another. However, Nehemiah refused to stop the work (Neh. 4). God had given him a mission, and he was not about to cave in to fear. The enemy of your soul is relent-less. He will push against you with words of doubt, seeking to make you think that you are incapable of doing the work God has called you to do or that you have misunderstood the Lord in some way.

When his enemies conspired against him, Nehemiah's faith held strong. He wrote,

> We prayed to our God, and because of them we set up a guard against them day and night. . . . Our enemies said, "They will not know or see until we come among them, kill them and put a stop to the work."
>
> When the Jews who lived near them came and told us ten times, "They will come up against us from every place where you may turn,"

then I stationed men in the lowest parts of the space behind the wall, the exposed places, and I stationed the people in families with their swords, spears and bows.

When I saw their fear, I rose and spoke to the nobles, the officials and the rest of the people: "Do not be afraid of them; remember the Lord who is great and awesome, and fight for your brothers, your sons, your daughters, your wives and your houses."

When our enemies heard that it was known to us, and that God had frustrated their plan, then all of us returned to the wall, each one to his work. (Neh. 4:9, 11–15)

Notice what Nehemiah *did not* do. He did not panic, become fearful or cynical, or pack his bags for home. He ignored the enemy's threats because he had been given a mandate by God to rebuild the city's walls.

You may think, *He knew what God wanted him to do.* However, you can know the same thing. God's will and purpose for your life are not hidden. You do not have to guess about the future. If you will pray and seek God's direction, He will provide it.

Usually fear comes when we feel unsure about our circumstances. Remember how the disciples reacted to the storm that threatened their lives on the Sea of Galilee?

Mark told us that Jesus had been teaching parables most of the day. While He was fully God, He also was a man who was subject to some of the same physical limitations that we face. He was tired, and as He climbed into a waiting boat along the shore of Galilee, He told His disciples, "Let us go over to the other side" (Mark 4:35).

Mark wrote, "Leaving the crowd, they took Him along with them in the boat, just as He was; and other boats were with Him. And there arose a fierce gale of wind, and the waves were breaking over the boat so much that the boat was already filling up. Jesus Himself was in the stern, asleep on the cushion" (vv. 36–38).

Imagine what it felt like to have the Son of God asleep in your boat. Yet these men forgot the power of the Man who was with them. They panicked. The moment they felt extremely threatened, they became fearful.

They were seasoned fishermen. They knew what it was like to be in a storm on the Sea of Galilee, and they knew that this was no ordinary storm. It was not threatening to the Savior, however.

Some of the storms buffeting you will be greater than anything you can imagine. You will want to cry out with the disciples, "Do You not care that I am perishing?"

God does care, and He wants us to learn how to respond to fear when it comes. His plan is not for us to crumble with feelings of anxiety. Instead, He wants us to know that He is aware of what is taking place. He also has our very best in mind. Though troubles come, He promises to bring good out of each one (Rom. 8:28).

How did Jesus want these men to respond to this fearful situation?

He wanted them to know that He was aware of their circumstances, even though it appeared that He was asleep. His eternal, sovereign, infinite, loving care for them was not hampered in any way by the circumstances. He was in control of the wind, the rain, and the sea. He was God in the flesh, and He knew exactly what was going on around their small boat. The same is true when it comes to your life.

He wanted them to come to Him in faith, not in fear. He wasn't surprised by their fear, and He certainly made it clear that He was God. Mark continued, "[The disciples] woke Him and said to Him, 'Teacher, do You not care that we are perishing?' And [Jesus] got up and rebuked the wind and said to the sea, 'Hush, be still.' And the wind died down and it became perfectly calm. And He said to them, 'Why are you afraid? Do you still have no faith?'" (Mark 4:38–40). How many times has each one of us wanted to cry out, "God, don't You care that I'm hurting and afraid?"

The storm may be raging around you. You may have lost your job or just received news that you have a serious illness. Your heart is beating fast at the thought, and you don't know what you will do. God does, and though it may seem that He is silent or "asleep," He's not. The psalmist assured us: "He who keeps you will not slumber" (Ps. 121:3).

Therefore, you can trust Him to keep you steady when the storms of life blow hard against you. Victory over fear comes when you learn to focus on the Savior and His instructions to you. Before the journey, Jesus told the disciples that they were "going over to the other side" of the lake. He had a destination in mind, and He also had a principle He wanted them to learn and follow.

Jesus may have gone to sleep, but He also allowed the storm to grow in magnitude so that the men would admit their only help was in Him. Once they did this, He stood up and commanded the wind and the waves to hush and to be still (Mark 4:39). Perhaps you need the Savior to do the same for you. If so, He will.

THROUGH THE VALLEY

David wrote, "Even though I walk through the valley . . ." (Ps. 23:4).

Jesus told His disciples, "Let us go over to the other side" (Mark 4:35).

God instructed Joshua, "Be strong and courageous, for you shall give this people possession of the land" (Josh. 1:6).

Words such as *but* and *what if* do not work with statements like these. Joshua knew better than to argue with God. Forty years earlier he had seen the results of negative reasoning, doubtful thinking, and fearful projections (Num. 13–14).

That was when Israel first stood at the gateway to the land God promised to give them. At that time, fear overwhelmed their hearts. Instead of going in and claiming what God had given, they became fearful and refused to obey the Lord. What was at the core of their unfounded fears?

- a lack of faith in God
- a lack of trust in His provision
- ignorance of His presence
- dismissal of His eternal protection
- oversight of His unconditional love

When you ignore the sovereignty and the awesome providential care of God, you will end up struggling with fear. You may ask, "Did God know I was going to get fired at work?" The answer is yes. Then the question shifts: "Why didn't He do something to stop this from happening?"

We must never forget a simple truth: though trouble comes from time to time and changes the landscape of our lives, God never changes (Heb. 13:8). He is faithful, and we can leave the thought of fear behind because He is in control. He is with us, beside us, and in us through the presence of the Holy Spirit (Matt. 28:20). He has promised to guide us, lead us, and bring us through one trial after another.

The prophet Isaiah wrote,

> The LORD will continually guide you,
> And satisfy your desire in scorched places,
> And give strength to your bones;
> And you will be like a watered garden,
> And like a spring of water whose waters do not fail. (Isa. 58:11)

Fear does not fit who you are. There may be moments when you feel panic; for example, you are driving and suddenly a car is headed straight toward you, or you receive news that a loved one has died. That is when you need to claim God's most precious promises.

One is in Romans 8:28: "We know that God causes all things to work together for good to those who love God, to those who are called according to His purpose." His calling is that we would trust Him, live for Him, commit our lives to Him, and allow Him to guide us to a place where He can use us for His glory. When we are in step with His will, He will not allow problems to overcome us.

How does fear become an issue in a person's life?

Fear can come as a result of the way we were raised. Without knowing the damage they are doing, parents may trigger a fearful response within our hearts. When I was a young man, my mother always cautioned me to be careful.

Like most parents, she was simply training me to be careful, especially while I was delivering newspapers. Regularly she would call out to me to look out for cars and "not to get hit." Because she never learned to swim, she would also say, "Don't get too close to deep water." It took a long time for me to learn to swim because I was scared of water. You could make a list of things that others have told you not to do as a result of some fear in their own lives.

Growing up, I was afraid of the dark. At some point, someone may have said something to me that caused me to feel fearful when the lights were turned out. I remember nights when I went to sleep with the bedcovers pulled over my head.

There came a point when I grew tired of cowering in fear. Whenever I felt fearful, I would pray. If it was dark and I had to deliver newspapers, I prayed for God's safety and protection. Soon fear began to vanish. Over a period of time, I grew to trust God in a greater way. I did not even think about whether it was dark or light. I was focused on the Lord.

This one habit helped to set a pattern for my life, which is to get up and pray every morning before I begin my activities. I could never thank God enough for my struggle with fear because it was the catalyst that led me into a closer relationship with Him. Consider this possibility: God may have allowed you to feel fearful to reveal more of Himself to you.

We struggle with fear because we allow our imaginations to go to places that God never intended us to visit. Most of the events that we fear never come true. Our fears are unfounded. While we worry about impending failure, death, and destruction, Satan is smiling because he knows he has our full attention. Whatever has your attention has you.

Our imagination is one of the most powerful gifts God has given us. Every bridge, building, or great structure that was ever designed began as a thought in someone's imagination.

God completely holds you and your life within His hand, and He will not allow anything to happen that is not a part of His will or purpose. The psalmist wrote,

> You have also given me the shield of Your salvation,
> And Your right hand upholds me;
> And Your gentleness makes me great.
> You enlarge my steps under me,
> And my feet have not slipped. (Ps. 18:35–36)

Sometimes we make choices that are outside His will and purpose for our lives. When we do this, we usually face the consequences of our decisions. Even then, though, God is at work in our lives. When we turn to Him and admit where we have gone wrong, He lifts us up emotionally and begins to give us the encouragement to get through the problem.

Ignorance of the promises in God's Word leads to fear. Far too many people have forgotten the emotional power available to them through God's promises. For example, many struggle with fear when it comes to their salvation. They have based their lives on feelings and at times may feel as though they are no longer saved by the grace of God.

I grew up in a church where I was taught to trust the Lord Jesus Christ as Savior. However, if you sinned, you would lose your salvation and possibly die and go to hell. You had to deal with your sin quickly or pay the price of being a sinner all over again.

One day, God began to speak to my heart and showed me that He died for my sins once and for all. In other words, He saved me based on my faith in Him and my desire for Him to be my Savior. My salvation was secure because He had paid the eternal price for my sin—past, present, and future. The author of Hebrews wrote, "Therefore He is able also to save forever those who draw near to God through Him, since He always lives to make intercession for them" (Heb. 7:25).

Paul instructed us with these words: "For as many as are the promises of God, in Him they are yes; therefore also through Him is our Amen to the glory of God through us. Now He who establishes us with you in Christ and anointed us is God, who also sealed us and gave us the Spirit in our hearts as a pledge" (2 Cor. 1:20–22). He also wrote, "He made Him [Jesus] who knew no sin to be sin on our behalf, so that we might become the righteousness of God in Him" (2 Cor. 5:21). Jesus actually took our place on the cross. God demands a payment for sin, and the only One capable of making this payment was His Son, the holy Lamb of God (John 1:29).

The Holy Spirit is God's personal pledge of salvation to us (2 Cor. 1:20–22; 5:5). In fact, His presence through the Spirit demonstrates His eternal commitment to us. This also reaffirms that He plans to complete the good work He has begun in our lives (Phil. 1:6). It is a promise we can claim. God would never send His Spirit to live in our lives only to rescind the decision. Once you have accepted Jesus Christ as your Savior, you are saved and sealed with His Spirit forever.

Finally, fear is often the result of a poor self-image. When a person feels inadequate or unprepared, or does not measure up to others, a sense of fear will surround his life. Fear vanishes when we begin to understand several things about God:

- He is not looking for us to perform a certain way. God is not looking for us to do a certain thing to experience His goodness, love, and mercy. These are the gifts He gives freely to those who come to know Him as Savior and Lord. He will never pull out a tape measure and measure the context of your life. He knows you and loves you with an eternal love that is not based on anything other than what His Son did for you on Calvary's cross. You can serve on committees, visit the sick, and take blankets to the homeless shelter, but if you do not know the personal love of God through His Son, all of that counts for nothing.

The same is true for those who already know Him. Today, especially in our works-orientated society, people want to do works to achieve entrance into heaven. The gift of God's salvation does not come this way. It is a gift of grace—one that we do not deserve—but one that is freely given by God to those who believe in His Son. Service and worship are two very important aspects of your Christian walk, but doing more of one or the other does not mean your reward in heaven or status on earth will be greater.

- We are adequate through Jesus Christ. He is the source of our strength and our living hope. When He calls us to do a certain task, He equips us. Moses had no idea that he could actually lead the nation of Israel out of Egyptian bondage. On his own, he could not. However, God promised to be with him throughout the entire journey: "And [the Lord] said, 'Certainly I will be with you, and this shall be the sign to you that it is I who have sent you: when you have brought the people out of Egypt, you shall worship God at this mountain'" (Ex. 3:12). God does not direct us to reach a certain goal and then abandon us in the middle of the process. If He calls us, He assumes responsibility for our completing the mission.

- We need to ask God to give us the right perspective. A poor self-image is the result of not seeing yourself the way God views you. From His way of thinking, there are no lost causes, no hopeless situations, and no one beyond His reach. How do you change the way you see yourself? Ask God to show you through His Word His view of you. You will be surprised and encouraged to learn that regardless of your past sins, limited education, or any number of self-esteem roadblocks, God is interested only in your love and devotion.

He does not love you based on anything you have or have not done. His love is based on one thing: His Son's death on Calvary's cross. That was where the penalty for your transgression was paid and where sin's power over your life was shattered. You can say no to defeating thoughts that lead to low self-esteem because God is the One who works through you. Your responsibility is to say yes to Him and then be willing to follow Him.

To change your perspective, you must learn to see yourself in light of God's power and possibilities. Peter was no more than a fisherman when Jesus called him to become one of His disciples. Matthew was a tax collector and, at the time, one of the most hated individuals in Jewish society because of his connection with the Roman government. Plus, tax collectors were notorious for adding extra tariffs to pad their own purses. Yet when Matthew met the Savior, he turned away from that lifestyle and assumed a new role—one that changed his view of himself. If you are struggling with feelings of low self-esteem, ask God to help you apply the truth found in the Gospels to your life so that you might walk in victory and hope as these men did.

CONSIDER THE CONSEQUENCES

There are many consequences of sin, and an obvious outcome of fear is *a divided mind.* The focus of our thoughts is no longer sure and steadfast—set on Christ. Instead, it is fragmented by thoughts of our circumstances, and we find it hard to concentrate on what God has called us to do.

If you are afraid, you will not be willing to take risks. And if you are living a godly life, you will face times when the only option left to you is to step out on faith, trusting God to provide a way for you to continue. Fear shouts, "What if you fail? Won't everyone laugh?"

During your lifetime, God will allow challenges and blessings to come that require nothing more than pure faith. You won't be able to see the next step in front of you. In fact, you may not even know what is coming around the next turn. The only option is to trust the one Person who knows all about you and all that you will encounter.

Procrastination is another consequence of fear. People become afraid of not doing something right. Therefore, they put off doing anything at all! I have listened as grown men have described how their parents told them that they would never amount to anything. Internally they believed this lie, and over the course of their lifetimes they began to procrastinate over the slightest activity. Yes, there was some fear of failure involved, but they also did not believe they could make a choice that was correct or meaningful. So rather than choose, they vacillated between any number of options.

Perhaps instead of encouraging a child to try a new activity, a parent persuaded his son not to try a task because he could fail or did not have the right ability. If you tell your daughter, "You will never amount to anything," you have laid the foundation for fear to grow in her life. You also have opened a wide door for Satan to come in and tempt her to be afraid of any new adventure.

One young woman told me how her father repeatedly told her that she would never achieve anything in life. Throughout her years in high school, she fulfilled his self-professed prophecy. Her grades were low and her choice of friends was questionable. She married immediately after graduation and several years later divorced. At each point of failure, her father's words appeared fresh in her memory. Finally, she cried out to God in desperation. She accepted Jesus Christ as her Savior, and her life changed dramatically. Within a very short period of time, she was involved in Christian work. She went to college, graduated at the top of her class, and ended up having a successful career working with missionaries who are preparing to go to the mission field.

"I ditched that negative way of thinking a long time ago. I never doubted my father's love even though it was very misguided. Once Christ came into my life, everything changed for the better. Through studying His Word, I learned that I could do anything He directed me to do. I guess Paul's words were right on target, 'I can do all things through Him who strengthens me'" (Phil. 4:13). At any point, this young woman could have given up. Negative comments can leave us feeling fearful and unable to achieve even the simplest task. The way to move past thoughts that seek to paralyze you with fear, doubt, and discouragement is to keep your eyes set on Christ. He believes in you even when others doubt your ability.

Instead of plotting a fearful path for our children to travel, we need to find ways to encourage them to believe that with God's help they can do anything. We limit God's work in their lives when we transfer our negative beliefs onto our children. We also risk stifling the creativity that God has placed within their hearts. One man admitted that he never thought he could achieve very much in life. Even though he had an opportunity to further his education, he did not take it. Instead, he returned home, married, and later went to work programming the minds of his children with negative thoughts. He often told his son, "You know, I never did well in school, and you are just like me." As if perfectly cued, the son grew up, entered college, and came home after a year.

When our hearts are full of fear, we won't try new adventures. This is because fear limits our ability to achieve the goals that God wants us to reach and enjoy. Countless people have never taken a risk because they are fearful and worry about what others will say should they fail. Here is the age-old truth about stepping out on faith: it is much better to try and fail than it is to shrink back in fear and live far below the level God has for you to live.

Fear undermines self-confidence. It is enslaving and can encompass your entire life. An older man admitted that he had spent his entire life battling an unseen fear. He really did not know how it began, but he knew it was there. He had a low-simmering sense of anxiety that prevented him from trying anything new. As a young man, he believed that God wanted him to enter the ministry, but his parents did not want him to leave them to go to school. Their greatest fear was that God could call him to the mission field and they would have no one.

What they had, instead, was a fearful grown man, who had never reached his full potential. Most of us know when we are yielding to fear. Each time the enemy tells us that we need to be afraid, we need to recall out loud the promises of God, beginning with 2 Timothy 1:7: "God has not given us a spirit of timidity [fear], but of power and love and discipline."

You cannot allow the fear of failure, rejection, or embarrassment to keep you from living life to the fullest. If you are faced with a challenge that seems greater than your ability to handle it, ask the Lord to affirm His will for your life through His Word. He will guide you, and if He wants you to go forward, then you can rest in the knowledge that He will never call you to do something without equipping you for the task.

When people ask, "What happens if God does not keep His promises?" I just shake my head in amazement. I want to ask them, "Do you mean that you are worried about God failing to keep a promise?" We never have to worry about this. He gives us His promises to encourage us and help us to stay focused on reaching our full potential.

GOD'S PROMISE TO YOU

In the book of Isaiah, the Lord gives us a wonderful promise of hope. To appreciate it, we need to understand that the nation of Israel was in a desperate state. The people's sin had driven them far from God.

It had also left them exposed to enemy attack and uncontrolled feelings of fear.

However, God had a strong word of encouragement and promise for them. Through the prophet Isaiah, He reminded the people that He had not forgotten them:

> " 'Do not fear, for I am with you;
> Do not anxiously look about you, for I am your God.
> I will strengthen you, surely I will help you,
> Surely I will uphold you with My righteous right hand.'
> Behold, all those who are angered at you will be shamed and
>   dishonored;
> Those who contend with you will be as nothing and will perish.
> You will seek those who quarrel with you, but will not find them,
> Those who war with you will be as nothing and non-existent.
> For I am the LORD your God, who upholds your right hand,
> Who says to you, 'Do not fear, I will help you.'" (Isa. 41:10–13)

Fear is a dreadful landmine. It is an uneasy feeling that something is not right—regardless of whether it is or not. Feelings of fear trigger an alarm within us that shouts a stiff warning. It also creates a swift sense of anxiety by telling us we are about to face something we may not know how to handle. There are real fears, perceived fears, and the fear of God, which is a reverent fear.

When I'm walking through the woods, which I often do as part of my hobby as a photographer, the last thing I want to hear is that unmistakable sound of a rattlesnake. If someone asked me, "Are you afraid of rattlesnakes?" I would answer yes without a moment's hesitation. I'm also afraid of black widow spiders. These are real fears. However, they do not control my life. I know that I can act in a healthy way to avoid situations that place me in contact with these creatures.

Some people take caution to the extreme, and fear grows in their hearts to a point where they no longer venture out to try new and exciting things. There is no way I would allow this caution to prevent me from enjoying the hobby I love, and the same should be true for you.

If you have a debilitating fear in a certain area, ask God to teach you how to keep it in check. Remember, even when life takes a sudden turn for the worse, God is sovereign and He promises to protect us (Jude 24). You may not realize it, but He is especially close when trouble comes. And He wants to calm your most restless fear so that like David, you will be able to walk through the valley knowing that He is right beside you.

We imagine something horrible is going to happen to us, and we will not be able to survive. Or we tell ourselves it will inflict such pain and sorrow in our lives that we will not be able to bear the suffering. God does not want us to live in fear. John reminded us, "There is no fear in love; but perfect love casts out fear, because fear involves punishment, and the one who fears is not perfected in love" (1 John 4:18).

To overcome fear, you must learn a simple principle that I have mentioned again and again in this book, and that is the principle of focus. When we keep our focus on Jesus Christ, life's struggles diminish and our faith becomes stronger.

When Joseph was betrayed by his brothers and sold into Egyptian captivity, he focused on the promises God had made to him. When David faced Goliath, he did not listen to the fearful words of his brothers and those who were in Israel's army. He focused only on God and won a tremendous victory.

Daniel emerged unscathed from the lions' den because he had spent the night praying to God for protection and deliverance. He was focused only on the Lord and not on the lions that tracked his every move with their eyes.

Paul, while a prisoner in Rome, focused on doing God's will, and an entire regiment in the Roman army came to know Jesus as Savior because he was intent on his mission and not his circumstances. He was not fixated on his discomforts or the fact he was chained to a

Roman soldier. His only goal was to do God's will. Often when we yield to fear, it is because our focus has shifted. Like the disciples during a raging storm on the Sea of Galilee, we cry out.

God has chosen you to fulfill His will. There is no one who can do what He has called you to do. Yet fear often prevents us from doing this because we are worried about our circumstances. "What if this goes wrong?" "I feel so badly and afraid, I shouldn't try. Something might happen to me or to someone I love. Then what would I do?" But Jesus says, "Do not be afraid, little flock, for your Father has chosen gladly to give you the kingdom" (Luke 12:32). Although fear may not be able to kill you physically, it can paralyze you and create such a deep sense of anxiety that you will become sick—emotionally and physically.

It is one of Satan's most powerful weapons, and he likes to use it against us at every opportunity. He watches our every step, looking for an opening in our emotions. When he sees one, he is quick to respond: "You need to be careful." "Don't do that. Let someone else try. You know what usually happens. If something can go wrong, it will happen to you." On and on his lies continue, and the landmines are set.

A NEW PERSPECTIVE

Joshua was a young man when God chose him to take Moses' place and lead the nation of Israel into the Promised Land. What an awesome responsibility he had been given. It was also a potential opportunity for fear. Moses would not be with him or the people as they entered the land. Israel had a new leader, and he needed to be encouraged and prepared for what was ahead. That was why God instructed him to "be strong and courageous" (Josh. 1:6).

There was only one way for Joshua to accomplish this, and it was by faith in God. If he allowed his emotions or thoughts to turn away from God, he would become overwhelmed by the task. There are times when we have something that we must do, and the only way to get through it is by setting the focus of our hearts on God and not on our circumstances. There was no way Joshua could lead the people into the land without God's help.

The Lord told him, "Only be strong and very courageous; be careful to do according to all the law which Moses My servant commanded you; do not turn from it to the right or to the left, so that you may have success wherever you go. . . . Have I not commanded you? Be strong and courageous! Do not tremble or be dismayed, for the LORD your God is with you wherever you go" (Josh. 1:7, 9).

If you want to defuse the landmine of fear, you must change the way you view the issues and struggles of life. You need to ask God to teach you how to view your life and circumstances from His perspective. God wanted Joshua to focus on

- the plan He had for the nation of Israel.
- the courage and strength available to him through faith in God.

Many times, conquering fear is just this simple: when a challenge comes, keep your focus on Christ and not on your circumstances. Notice that God did not deliver a lengthy speech about all that was waiting for Joshua in the land that would soon be their permanent home. He did not tell the nation's new leader about any future threat. He reminded His servant to remain faithful to the calling he had been given. Nothing else mattered.

If God has placed you in a certain position, He will handle all the details concerning it and your life. Your only responsibility is to obey Him and leave the consequences to Him.

In Psalm 61, the psalmist wrote,

> Lead me to the rock that is higher than I.
> For You have been a refuge for me,
> A tower of strength against the enemy.

Let me dwell in Your tent forever;

Let me take refuge in the shelter of Your wings. (vv. 2–4)

Then in Psalm 91, he reminded us of God's protective care,

He who dwells in the shelter of the Most High

Will abide in the shadow of the Almighty.

I will say to the LORD, "My refuge and my fortress,

My God, in whom I trust!"

For it is He who delivers you from the snare of the trapper

And from the deadly pestilence.

He will cover you with His pinions,

And under His wings you may seek refuge. . . .

You will not be afraid of the terror by night,

Or of the arrow that flies by day;

Of the pestilence that stalks in darkness,

Or of the destruction that lays waste at noon.

A thousand may fall at your side

And ten thousand at your right hand,

But it shall not approach you. . . .

For you have made the LORD, my refuge,

Even the Most High, your dwelling place.

No evil will befall you,

Nor will any plague come near your tent.

For He will give His angels charge concerning you,

To guard you in all your ways. (vv. 1–11)

An older woman admitted she did not venture out much at night, "Things happen," she said with a sigh, "and there are a lot of bad things that can happen." Being cautious is fine, but being fearful is not in keeping with God's plan for your life. Bad things can and do happen to anyone, at any time. Fear becomes a true problem when we focus on it. John wrote, "Perfect love [God's love] casts our fear" (1 John 4:18). When you have the love of God in your heart, you can overcome the landmine of fear because you have the greatest source of encouragement, hope, and strength living within you.

There is also a protective sense of fear that God provides. I can remember once being alone with a friend in the mountains and suddenly feeling very uneasy about our surroundings. We had become so engrossed in photographing the landscape, that we had become oblivious to everything else. We studied the area around us and it appeared safe, but we definitely felt we should hike back to the car. We did, and we also drove on to another location. I'm not sure why God prompted me to pack up and move; I was more than willing to act on His leading. But I did not feel that we should end the day. Instead, we traveled to the next stop and went on with our plans.

The woman mentioned above obviously had not learned to trust God the way the psalmist mentioned in the verses just cited. While we need to be cautious and discerning, many times the enemy can use thoughts of fear to prevent us from stepping out and enjoying the good things God gives.

The enemy is looking for a place in your life to bury his landmine. However, if you are proactive in the way you approach dangerous situations, he will not have the opportunity to do this. You cannot be careless. Instead, listen for the voice of the Spirit—not the voice of fear—to direct you. There is a huge difference. Fear is something the enemy chatters about. God will never use fear to instruct you. He may want you to fear Him, which is a reverent fear that honors and loves, but He will never prompt you to become anxious or fretful.

The Spirit of God may caution you to be careful, but when He does, He will provide the wisdom to avoid a dangerous situation. Fear sends panic racing through our hearts and emotions, paralyzing us and isolating us.

In 1 John 4:18–19, John wrote, "There is no fear in love; but perfect love casts out fear, because fear involves punishment, and the one who fears is not perfected in love. We love, because [God] first loved us." When we walk in the light of God's love and not in the darkness of fear, we will sense the difference. From time to time, God will allow waves of fear to break across our bows. He does this to demonstrate His love and strength toward us, but He also allows us to encounter difficulty to reveal the level of our faith.

There is a sure way through dark, fearful valleys, and that is to walk by faith, not by sight (2 Cor. 5:7). In fact, when you keep your heart set on Christ, you will be able to say with many of the godly saints who have gone before you that trials and difficulties are the evidence of God's nearness and earnest desire to draw us closer to Himself.

Remember, Satan places the landmine of fear with a single purpose, and that is to divide our minds so we will fail in our faith. Faith, however, keeps us unified with God and strengthens us in times of emergency, trial, and sorrow. No fear, no threat, no challenge is greater than His ability to conquer it. And His power is alive within the life of everyone who believes in Him.

A TIME TO MOVE FORWARD

For many people, fear is an addiction. Some even gain attention by telling others about their fears. They are fearful about the future along with their health, finances, and jobs. They are stuck, and there is only one way to get out of the disastrous rut they are in: they must admit there is a deep problem. Doing this can be difficult, though, because fear is a source of security for some people.

If you are fearful, you don't have to try a new challenge. You can just proclaim that you are living life simply and you are content being who you are—locked away in your safe environment. While we don't need to be compulsively driven to take on one new challenge after another, we need to seek ways to be used by God to lead others into a personal relationship with His Son. Giving in to fear will prevent us from stepping out of our comfort zone to serve God better.

"I'm just a fearful person," one man told me. My advice to him was to admit his fears to the Lord and ask for His help in working through each one.

Recently a nightly news program reported how a young soldier lost his foot in a landmine incident in Iraq. He returned home to heal, but he quickly realized, for him, emotional healing could be found only on the battlefield. Therefore, after his physical recovery, he asked to be sent back to Iraq. He became the first soldier to return to a combat position after losing a limb. He later told a reporter, "I wanted to face my fears, and this was the place to do it." This needs to be a rule that each one of us follows. In fact, God wants us to capitalize on our fears by not allowing them to control us. Instead, we can learn to use them as stepping-stones to a higher level of faith in Christ as we trust Him to guide us, keep us safe, and provide for our needs.

We begin each day on the battlefield of life. The enemy plants a series of landmines in our path, hoping that we will step on one that will explode and keep us from accomplishing God's will and purpose. You can overcome fear when you do the following:

- *Admit there is a problem and you need God's help.* There is something immensely powerful about admitting, "God, I am hurting. I feel fearful, and I know it is the enemy's desire to stop me from being successful. Please help me to hear Your voice and Your words of encouragement."

- *Confess your belief in God's sovereign care.* Every fear is shattered on a single truth: God is sovereign, and He will not leave us in what appears to be a helpless situation. He has the advantage of knowing all things and seeing every problem or challenge from every angle. He is all-powerful and never hesitates to give us the wisdom we need for every situation.

After the crucifixion, the disciples went into hiding. Terror gripped their hearts. They were sure that they would be arrested for following Jesus and crucified for their faith. Fear tempts us to go beyond a rational point in our minds where we know that God cares for us. Jesus had made it clear that He would have to die, but He would return to them. In the heat of battling fear, they forgot His promise to them and fled to the upper room where they remained until He appeared to them (Luke 24:36–39; John 14:3–4, 18–21).

- *Commit yourself to spending time each day with God in prayer.* The single most important activity you can do each day is to pray. Nothing carries the value that this does. Reading and studying God's Word are just as important, but it is in prayer that you learn to worship God and hear His voice speaking to you through His Word and the presence of the Holy Spirit.

 Each one of us needs to maintain a godly sense of fear. It is a reverent fear for God that reflects our desire to worship, honor, and obey Him. We recognize that He is holy and worthy of all our praise. The psalmist wrote, "O fear the LORD, you His saints; / For to those who fear Him there is no want" (Ps. 34:9). And the author of Proverbs reminded us, "The fear of the LORD is the beginning of wisdom" (Prov. 9:10).

- *Meditate on God's Word, which contains His personal promises to you.* You can seal fear's fate in your life by studying and meditating on God's Word. The truth that is found in the Bible dismantles fear and brings an immeasurable sense of hope. God told Joshua,

Every place on which the sole of your foot treads, I have given it to you, just as I spoke to Moses. . . . No man will be able to stand before you all the days of your life. Just as I have been with Moses, I will be

183

with you; I will not fail you or forsake you. Be strong and courageous, for you shall give this people possession of the land. (Josh. 1:3, 5–6)

Joshua had this promise from God, and he carried it in his heart. When trouble came, he could remind the Lord what He promised.

People who do not read and study God's Word are like ships without rudders. They may be floating, but there is no real sense of direction in their lives. When you have God's Word hidden in your heart, the Spirit will immediately bring a verse of Scripture to mind when sorrow, disappointment, or fear come.

For example, you may face a serious threat. If you have read and meditated on God's Word, the Holy Spirit may remind you of the words in Psalm 27:

> The LORD is my light and my salvation;
> Whom shall I fear?
> The LORD is the defense of my life;
> Whom shall I dread? . . .
> Though a host encamp against me,
> My heart will not fear;
> Though war arise against me,
> In spite of this I shall be confident. (vv. 1, 3)

Or you could claim the words written in Psalm 18:

> "I love You, O LORD, my strength."
> The LORD is my rock and my fortress and my deliverer,
> My God, my rock, in whom I take refuge;
> My shield and the horn of my salvation, my stronghold.
> I call upon the LORD, who is worthy to be praised,
> And I am saved from my enemies. (vv. 1–3)

In Psalm 46, the psalmist wrote,

> God is our refuge and strength,
> A very present help in trouble.
> Therefore we will not fear, though the earth should change
> And though the mountains slip into the heart of the sea. (vv. 1–2)

The only way to find true peace, confidence, and assurance is to receive the Lord Jesus Christ as your personal Savior. This includes confessing your sinfulness to Him and acknowledging that when He died on the cross, His death paid your sin-debt in full—absolutely and completely (John 3:15–16). The moment you ask Him to forgive you, He does. When you surrender your life to Him, He seals your eternal future with the Holy Spirit (John 14:25–26). This means that while you may face many obstacles, you do not have anything to fear because you are not alone. God has promised never to leave or forsake you (Deut. 31:6, 8). Fear vanishes when we apply the truth of God to our situation.

The enemy may whisper, "What if . . . ?" But you can answer with full assurance that you belong to Jesus Christ and He has a wonderful future planned for you. There is no age limit on this promise. The moment you place your trust in Him is the moment to take your first step toward eternal victory over fear.

TEN

THE LANDMINE OF IMMORALITY

The woman's eyes were fiery. She was determined more than convinced that her sinful lifestyle was acceptable. Actually, she could not stop talking about her sin as she sought to persuade her friends that what she was doing was okay. "After all," she said with a hint of pride in her voice, "I'm not hurting anyone. Besides, you are supposed to be Christians. God loves me, and He wouldn't condemn me. Neither should you."

Satan always seeks to tempt us to compromise by turning the tables on our belief system. In a way this woman was right; God does love her. However, her sin was a landmine of horrendous proportions. God hates sin. He loves the sinner, but He makes it very clear in His Word that sin is detestable to Him. The author of Proverbs wrote,

> Listen to me
> And do not depart from the words of my mouth.
> Keep your way far from [the adulteress]
> And do not go near the door of her house,
> Or you will give your vigor to others

And your years to the cruel one;

And strangers will be filled with your strength

And your hard-earned goods will go to the house of an alien;

And you groan at your final end,

When your flesh and your body are consumed;

And you say, "How I have hated instruction!

And my heart spurned reproof! (Prov. 5:7–12)

God has called us to live holy lives, but increasingly people walk to the beat of the culture of our day. It is a culture set on criticizing God and His Word, calling His values out of date and out of touch with reality. Nothing could be further from the truth, and Satan knows it. Yet he seeks to spread his wickedness by telling people the same old lie that snared Adam and Eve. It is a propositional lie that is misleading and dead wrong. It says, "There is more to enjoy in this life than what God wants you to experience."

The truth is, sin destroys us—if not physically, certainly emotionally and spiritually. Once again the author of Proverbs wrote,

Can a man take fire in his bosom

And his clothes not be burned?

Or can a man walk on hot coals

And his feet not be scorched? (Prov. 6:27–28)

We may try to justify our actions in numerous ways, but we cannot change the principles in God's Word.

The landmine of sexual sin always results in disastrous consequences. There are sins, and then there are devastating sins. Sexual sin is destructive in a massive way. In the first stages, it may seem to be nothing more than a habit or a temptation. But it is quickly addictive and always creates deep sorrow in the lives of those involved. In most cases, this includes family members, friends, coworkers, and many more.

You cannot eliminate the consequences of sexual sin, because when this landmine explodes, it has the potential to bring destruction to every area of a person's life.

THE NATURE OF IMMORALITY

You may be at a crossroads in your life where you think it would be more enjoyable to live the way you choose rather than follow God's principles. The last thing you want is someone telling you what you should or should not do.

If this is the case, then you need to know that true peace, joy, and contentment always elude those who chase after sin. Solomon found this to be true, and he wrote,

> All that my eyes desired I did not refuse them. I did not withhold my heart from any pleasure, for my heart was pleased because of all my labor and this was my reward for all my labor. Thus I considered all my activities which my hands had done and the labor which I had exerted, and behold all was vanity and striving after wind and there was no profit under the sun. (Eccl. 2:10–11)

Solomon had everything—concubines, slaves, houses, vineyards, silver, gold, stables filled with horses, and much more. Yet he said all of this was nothing more than wind passing through his hands. His accomplishments brought only a sense of emptiness to his heart because the things he valued the most had nothing to do with God.

When I think about the whole issue of sexual sin, I also think about the emptiness, heartache, and disappointment it brings. There is no way for me to express the sorrow I have witnessed over the years as a result of people falling prey to Satan's entrapments.

Our families are under attack along with the traditional view of marriage. All of this can be traced to the deterioration of godly values in our homes, churches, and schools. Today people are more concerned about what society thinks is correct than what God says is right.

Passions are out of control. People have become involved in relationships purely to fulfill lustful desires. When the relationship ends, they are left with feelings of deep loneliness, betrayal, emotional abuse, and failure. Society may tell you, "Live any way you please." But no one will mention that God has the final word concerning sin and its consequences. Once sin has had its way, God is the only One willing to pick up the shattered pieces of your life. The world does not comfort failures—people who are outcasts or hopelessly given over to addiction and passions that are out of control.

Guilt digs at the heart of the person enslaved by sin. It haunts the person who cannot stay away from the coworker and insists on meeting her after work, even though his wife is at home with his children waiting for him. At first sin appears to be an adventure, but it quickly becomes a place of high anxiety, secrecy, and worry.

God forbids adultery, debauchery, fornication, homosexuality, and anything that violates His moral law and principles. One's inner conscience knows this. However, people often ignore the very warning signs their consciences produce. They work overtime to hide the very things that are eating them up inside, such as pornography, rape, sexual abuse, and such.

Recently we have witnessed one sexual scandal come to light after another. Lives are shattered by sin. Families are being torn apart by actions of people who are out of control.

Some proclaim they are living a gay lifestyle, but nothing is happy or gay about the destructive behavior of homosexuality. Anything that opposes the principles written in God's Word leads to one ending— the end Solomon mentioned, a place of extreme emptiness where wind and sorrow breach the soul. Ultimately it ends in a place of extreme emotional sorrow and separation from God.

Over the years, people have asked me if their sin would prevent them from going to heaven. The one thing that prevents us from experiencing eternal salvation is the refusal to accept Christ as Savior and Lord.

We may fall into sin, but if we truly know Him, we will not remain there. Sin and God's holiness have no common ground. God is holy, and He cannot look on sin. He will hear the prayer of a sinner, but He never accepts the sin someone purposefully commits.

Paul wrote, "God has not called us for the purpose of impurity, but in sanctification. So, he who rejects this is not rejecting man but the God who gives His Holy Spirit to you" (1 Thess. 4:7–8). The Lord takes full responsibility for commanding us to live godly lives. Sanctification is a process that continues over time. It means that we are becoming more like Christ. The more we surrender our lives to God, the more He shapes us into the image of His Son. We are sanctified, made holy, through our relationship with Him. Salvation is a one-time event, but sanctification is something that takes place over a lifetime. When we accept Christ as our Savior, He saves us from the penalty of our sin. He forgives us. He also declares us not guilty of sin, because He has forgiven our past, present, and future transgressions. Therefore, in the future when we sin, we begin to learn about the consequences of our actions and how we can avoid future failures.

We are saved by His grace immediately, but we are being sanctified through our faith in Christ. It is an ongoing process, because we spend our entire lives learning how to live the Christian life and how to reflect His love and goodness to others. It is a journey of faith, but one that also leads to holiness of heart and a deeper level of purity.

THINGS WE NEED TO ADMIT

As we talked about earlier, God walks step-by-step with us. We are in the process of becoming like Him. As long as our hearts are turned toward Him, we should look more like His Son and less like the wickedness of the world around us. In Exodus 20:14, God told the nation of Israel, "You shall not commit adultery." His principles are just that simple.

Sin is an enticement to disobey almighty God. It is an invitation to rebel against Him in some way. Sin also is universal. Paul wrote, "No temptation has overtaken you but such as is common to man; and God is faithful, who will not allow you to be tempted beyond what you are able, but with the temptation will provide the way of escape also, so that you will be able to endure it" (1 Cor. 10:13).

Everyone, at some point, will face Satan's temptation. We must remember, however, that while he may tempt us to disobey God, we can say no. The Lord has given us exactly what we need to resist the enemy—the power of His Word and the presence of His Holy Spirit. When Jesus was tempted to disobey the Lord, He used God's Word to rebuke the enemy's pursuit.

God also has promised to provide a way of escape. The problem is that too many people do not take it. They actually believe that they can take a step in sin's direction and not get burned. Over the years, I have heard many people say, "I can quit anytime I want to," but what they quickly discover is that they can't. This is because of the foundational nature of sin. It was ignited by Satan to destroy our lives and testimony, and the enemy will not stop tempting us until he has reached his goal.

People often ask me, "What does 'shall not' mean?" (review Ex. 20:14). It means there is to be no rationalization, no redefining, camouflaging, compromise, or attempt at making what God says is wrong to become right. Adultery is wrong, and the consequences are serious. It carries with it a hefty price tag.

God tells us in Leviticus 20:10, "If there is a man who commits adultery with another man's wife, one who commits adultery with his friend's wife, the adulterer and the adulteress shall surely be put to death." Over the years, we have changed the face of adultery to a point that it now wears a mask of romantic love. God said to put the persons involved to death! That demonstrates how firm He was with anything that tempted His people to become unfaithful and disloyal to their marriage vows. He knew the consequences of sin.

GOD'S JUDGMENT AND GOD'S GRACE

We can go straight back to the Garden of Eden for a glimpse of the destructive power of sin. One action, one lie, one moment of sin ended in unspeakable sorrow. It also led to the detonation of a landmine that changed all that Adam and Eve knew as good and pleasurable.

In Leviticus 20 we read, "If there is a man who lies with a male as those who lie with a woman, both of them have committed a detestable act; they shall surely be put to death" (v. 13). It does not get any plainer than this. God hates sin, but our society wants to deny this and says, "Well, that was the Old Testament. Today we are living in a time of grace."

It is true that we are living under the grace of God's love, but this does not mean we can ignore the laws of God. Paul wrote,

> For this reason God gave them over to degrading passions; for their women exchanged the natural function for that which is unnatural, and in the same way also the men abandoned the natural function of the woman and burned in their desire toward one another, men with men committing indecent acts and receiving in their own persons the due penalty of their error. And just as they did not see fit to acknowledge God any longer, God gave them over to a depraved mind, to do those things which are not proper. (Rom. 1:26–28)

God has placed principles within His Word to guide us and to protect us. He knows the consequences of sin. He also knows that we reap what we sow, more than we sow, and later than we sow. Some consequences of sin continue for a long time. In fact, some may be with us an entire lifetime.

Again Paul wrote, "Do you not know that the unrighteous will not inherit the kingdom of God? Do not be deceived; neither fornicators, nor idolaters, nor adulterers, nor effeminate, nor homosexuals, nor thieves, nor the covetous, nor drunkards, nor revilers, nor swindlers, will inherit the kingdom of God" (1 Cor. 6:9–10).

A person who is deeply engaged in sin may not die physically, though some of the sins that are committed can lead to this very end. But one thing is certain: he or she will face a spiritual, emotional, and mental death. Physicians' offices are filled to overflowing with people who are struggling with sin, disobedience, and rebellion. Their lives reflect an agitating presence of anxiety or a sorrowful countenance of depression. They don't understand why they are battling feelings of guilt and anger every day. It is the result of sin—rebellion against God.

"If I could just have an hour of peace," one woman sighed. Her life was in shambles, and she refused to give her life to Jesus Christ. She wanted to hang on to what she believed was a sense of freedom, and she openly admitted that she did not want anyone to tell her what to do.

She was determined to live her life the way she planned. No matter how many relationships she had in the past or how large her bank account became, she did not have true peace. And she knew it. It wasn't until she surrendered to the unconditional love of God that she had her first peaceful night's sleep in a very long time.

When you are tempted by sin, remember Satan has a goal for your life—destruction. Sin is the best way he can achieve this. He also will use feelings of depression, guilt over past sins that have been forgiven by God, and anxiety to prevent you from experiencing God's blessings.

The world's message is: it's your life; do whatever you want to do. Many have tried this and have ended up living each day with a foreboding sense of sorrow and regret.

Christ's message is: "Truly, truly, I say to you, everyone who commits sin is the slave of sin. . . . [However,] if the Son makes you free, you will be free indeed" (John 8:34, 36). There is only one way to be free from sin, and that is through faith in Jesus Christ. At times, sin may be so addictive that a person will need professional help. Yet if there is knowledge of God's unconditional acceptance and love, emotional healing and freedom from bondage are easier to establish.

All sexual sin begins like any other temptation—in the mind with a thought. From a thought it moves into the imagination. A person will imagine what a certain experience would be like. Usually there is a sense of identification with the other person involved. A desire begins to grow until it becomes constant and strong. You can deal with sin at any point up to this moment. As I mentioned earlier, you can also say no and turn and walk away.

However, if you allow the feelings to continue, they will become a fantasy and a part of who you are. Soon it will seem normal to act on your feelings. Sexual sin is like nothing else you will face. It is all-consuming, but God can break the bondage of the deepest sin.

You will need to admit that you need His help and His deliverance. If you don't deal with sin, it will deal with you.

THE UNDERLYING CAUSES OF SIN

Almost every day we will meet people who appear to be happy. They have good jobs, nice homes, and lots of friends. Deep inside, where only God can see, however, an addictive fire is raging. It is a wicked blaze that threatens to consume them along with every hope and dream they have.

James wrote, "Each one is tempted when he is carried away and enticed by his own lust" (James 1:14). We cannot blame anyone else for our sin. Nevertheless, many people seek to do this very thing. After all, remember Adam's answer to God when He asked, "Have you eaten from the tree of which I commanded you not to eat?" (Gen. 3:11). Adam replied, "The woman whom You gave to be with me, she gave me from the tree, and I ate" (v. 12). In a single interchange, Adam blamed not only his wife but also God for his failure to follow instructions.

The temptation was not too great for him to handle had he turned to God and asked for help. But he didn't because he wanted to see if what the enemy was telling him was true. It was to a degree—his eyes were opened to the reality of sin, death, and sorrow, such as he had never experienced.

God never changes. His principles and promises remain steadfast. Therefore, a moral law that is stated in the Old Testament is just as valid in the New Testament.

The apostle Paul virtually restated the moral principle of the book of Exodus in 1 Corinthians: "Flee immorality. Every other sin that a man commits is outside the body, but the immoral man sins against his own body. Or do you not know that your body is a temple of the Holy Spirit who is in you, whom you have from God, and that you are not your own? For you have been bought with a price: therefore glorify God in your body" (1 Cor. 6:18–20).

God created us. Our bodies belong to Him and not to us. We can treat them immorally, but this does not change the fact that He created us. He gave us life for a purpose, and that was to bring glory and honor to His name. He desires our fellowship. Even though we have sinned deeply against Him, God still loves each one of us.

Earlier, I discussed the life of the woman at the well (John 4:7–29). She was entrapped by sin. Over her young lifetime, she had been married several times. When Jesus met her, the man she was living with was not her husband. Her life was going nowhere.

We have to wonder if she felt like giving up. She was drawing water in the middle of the day—something that no decent woman did. Women in that time did not go to the well at midday. She was there, more than likely, to avoid contact with other women. There was a sense of shame and guilt. If not, she would have been with the others—laughing and talking. But she was alone.

The Savior offered her an eternal gift, which was exactly what her heart and soul had longed to receive. Sin is no longer an option after we accept God's love and forgiveness.

PRINCIPLES TO LIVE BY

God has given us foundational principles, boundaries, and guidelines to follow. If we violate them, we will reap the consequences. Sexual fulfillment is reserved for marriage. It is something to be enjoyed between a husband and wife—not two men and not two women.

It also should be something that flows from a sense of genuine love—godly love for one's spouse. It may be an act of love, but it also reflects our willingness to ask, "What is best for my wife?" or "What is best for my husband?" Sexual expression should be unselfish, intimate, and most of all, based on God's love.

This is certainly not the world's view of sex. The prevailing attitude of much of our society is to take all that you can and never think about the consequences. But there *are* consequences. Foremost is the fact that when we disobey God, our hearts and minds become darkened—blinded to His joy and deaf to His goodness. Never forget: sin may seem fun for a season, but soon the truth emerges. The newness wears off, and we are left to deal with the broken pieces created by our disobedience.

Satan crouches at our door, waiting for us to appear interested in some behavior that is sinful and dead wrong. At times, he tells us that we have needs and those needs must be met. If given an opportunity, he will bombard a person's mind with thoughts of passion until it seems he is being driven by an unseen force—one that beckons him to meet his needs without consideration of God's will.

Again there is a degree of truth within this lie. God has created each one of us with basic needs. Sexual fulfillment or intimacy is one of these.

However, many people who are not married find fulfillment in ways other than sexual expression. Problems arise when a person goes against the moral principles God has established in His Word. He created sex so that we could express love to our spouses.

It has been heartbreaking to me to listen to the many accounts of infidelity. Young men and women thought that the only way they could experience love was to engage in sexual contact without waiting to be married. Others strayed in their love for one another and ended up in adulterous relationships—all because they listened to Satan's lie and believed that there was something better than what God had given them.

This may sound old-fashioned, but if you fail to wait until you are married to express your love for your mate, then you will miss one of the most precious blessings that God has given to every man and woman. There is something about purity and the marriage bed that lifts a relationship to a higher level.

CONTINUING CONSEQUENCES OF SIN

There is another group of people who suffer more than they admit. These are the ones who make a horrendous mistake of believing that if they will just go to bed with another person, they will find the intimacy and love that their hearts long to experience.

Secular psychologists have long suggested that sex outside marriage leads to feelings of guilt, shame, and low self-esteem. Christian counselors know this is true, because sexual intimacy is the most private expression two people can have for one another. It touches the core of a person, and if that touch is one of no commitment or lasting love, it can be devastating.

People misuse sex for many selfish reasons:

- to build personal self-esteem
- to meet personal desires

- to control another person

- to make financial gains (This includes prostitution.)

- to express lust and abuse

The man sitting across from me had refused to listen to the caution of his friends. He had been determined to carry on an affair, even though he was married. As a believer, he should have known better, but he had opened the door to sin through what seemed to be a harmless act of kindness at his job.

A coworker was hurting, and at first she just wanted to talk about her husband and the trouble they were having. He reassured her everything would work out and he would pray for her family. Soon they began to go to lunch together—just to talk. They laughed freely, and when confronted by another coworker, he became defensive and responded quickly: "We're just friends." His answer was spoken with enough force to back others away from mentioning the subject again.

After a few weeks, they decided to stay at the office a little later and then grab a bite to eat before heading home. Step-by-step they became emotionally involved to the point that he realized he was getting up in the morning thinking about the woman at his office and not about the wife he was leaving for the day. When his wife asked about his late evenings, he became more defensive. He began to think the only one who really knew and understood him was the woman at his office. By then, his peers were avoiding him and his friend. They knew what was about to happen, and some also knew how it would end.

A friend had tried one final time to convince the man that his actions were dead wrong. But the warning came too late. His mind was seared, made up, and engulfed in a desire to express his passion for this woman, which he evidently did—not once but many times—until his wife packed her bags and left.

Tears rolled down his face, and he could barely make eye contact with me because he finally realized the weight of his sin.

The consequences of sexual sin are many and very sobering. They include the following:

Guilt. An alarm goes off inside, signaling that what you have done is wrong. There is a sense of heaviness that cannot be easily satisfied. Too many people have lived with sin for so long that this alarm has become faint, if audible in their spirits at all.

Self-condemnation. The enemy will lead you into sin and then belittle you for acting on your sinful passions. Sin and condemnation can become a vicious cycle. The better your relationship with God, the more condemned you will feel because this is the nature of sin—to condemn God's children.

Anxiety. A believer will reach a point where he is anxious about his relationship with God. He knows sin has broken his fellowship, and a sense of anxiety is evidence of this.

Divided mind. The man in this story could not think clearly. He was blinded by his adulterous relationship. His work suffered along with all of his relationships. He began to forget simple things, such as fulfilling or meeting the needs of his family and friends. When sin is involved, everyone suffers.

Damaged self-esteem. By the end of the affair, this man felt horrible about what he had done. The enemy bombarded his mind with degrading words of failure and depression.

Feeling of hypocrisy. Sexual sin causes us to doubt who we are in Christ. When we do this, we will feel that we have failed and become fake in our walk with the Lord.

Deep sense of emptiness. Nothing satisfies our hearts and souls like the love of God. But where there is sin, loneliness and emptiness are sure to follow.

Disappointment and lack of contentment. One sign of deep sin within our lives is a growing discontentment. Often we see this escalating in a person's life, especially if that person is involved in sinful behavior. It is as if he is being driven by his sinful desires and does not have the ability to stop the very action that will lead to his ruin. In the aftermath of sin, disappointment consumes his heart because he thought the very thing he wanted would bring fulfillment. However, sin never brings fulfillment.

Feeling of dishonesty. People who become entrapped in transgressions will find it easy to lie without a hint of guilt, especially at first. "Honey, I have to work late. Don't wait on me for dinner." They may find words like these easy to say, but they will never know the heartache they bring to someone at home waiting for them.

Willful disobedience. Once you say yes to sin, it is easy to say yes again and again. Where there was once a check in your spirit cautioning you to stop, now there is nothing blocking your way. This is a tremendously dangerous place, because through disobedience a person chooses to reject God and His commandments. Essentially he is saying, "I know better than God," or "I know what I want to do and don't care what anyone says."

Unspeakable regret. Sin causes sorrow so deep that, for many, it is hard to move past. God promises that if we will confess our sins to Him, He will forgive and restore us (1 John 1:9). Some people spend a lifetime living in sin. When they grow old, they regret their actions.

Shame and guilt have taken their toll by leaving a wake of physical and emotional problems. However, neither can prevent God from loving you. There is always hope with God. The enemy may think that he has stolen your sense of hope, but God can and will restore it when you cry out to Him.

The author of Proverbs cautioned,

> The lips of an adulteress drip honey
> And smoother than oil is her speech;
> But in the end she is bitter as wormwood. . . .
> Her feet go down to death. . . .
> She does not ponder the path of life;
> Her ways are unstable, she does not know it. (Prov. 5:3–6)

Sin, lust, and out-of-control passion blind a person to the truth of God.

Doubt. Sin always creates doubt—doubt about your relationship to God, doubt concerning the future, doubt about your health, and doubt about how others view you.

Lack of effectiveness and time wasted. Because sin divides our minds, our effectiveness will diminish. Anytime you have sin within you, gnawing away at the core of who you are, you will waste time worrying about what will happen next or whether there will be a future.

Sin robs us of hope and purpose. Our focus shifts from God to ourselves—our actions, needs, and desires. Suddenly, instead of thinking about the Lord and others, we are caught up in our sinful actions, and there is no way we can continue to be effective at work, at home, or in our relationships.

Fear. There is a fear of pregnancy and perhaps an incurable disease in sexual sin. Fear is foundational to sin. When we are living in a right relationship to God, we can face difficulties and trials without becoming fearful. Once sin is involved, however, life becomes unsure, unstable, and unpredictable. God doesn't move, but we do. When we stop sensing His closeness, we become afraid that our lives are spinning out of control.

You can have a wonderful relationship with a person without becoming sexually involved until you exchange marriage vows. Far too many people fail to do this and end up suffering heartache and disappointment.

Broken relationships. Most of us have heard someone say, "What I'm doing won't hurt anyone but me." Sin hurts. It hurts the moral fabric of society. But more than this, it hurts the heart of God. It damages your relationship with Him because it creates an emotional wall that separates you from His love. Even though He doesn't stop loving you, He will not bless sin. And sin will prevent you from praying and living in fellowship with Him.

Sexual sin isolates a person from friends and family. When there is something to hide, we usually do not want others around. The enemy will tempt you to stay hidden by telling you that what you are feeling is special and no one else will understand. It also brings separation, because once the transgression is exposed, others will be shocked and hesitate to remain involved with you.

Damaged testimony. The testimonies of several Christian leaders have been permanently damaged as a result of sinful behavior. Ministries have been destroyed as the result of sinful passion and lust. Each one of us is responsible before God for his or her behavior.

We have all the truth we need to live godly lives. And the world is watching—waiting—to see if we will do it and remain faithful to the One who loves us with an everlasting love and who has promised never to leave us. There is no greater love than God's love.

I have also observed ministries undergo severe trials because leaders have not confronted sin. You must bring it to a halt and deal with it, or God will. Until you do this, He will set a limit on your usefulness. Many times, sin can be so extreme it will prevent a person from rising to the position God originally wanted him to hold. However, when there is true repentance, there is also restoration through Jesus Christ.

Sexual addiction. The numbers of those trapped by sexual addictions are on the rise. The Internet continues to compound the situation each year. Countless individuals think, *It won't hurt to take a quick look. I'm just going to join the online chat room for an hour or so. I can stop anytime.* The truth is: no, you can't. Once pornography or any sexually deviant behavior gains access to your mind, it will quickly build a stronghold—a power base from which sin and debauchery can operate. You may laugh at this and say, "Don't be silly. I'm in control." But you are not, because whatever has you—your thoughts and actions—will ultimately control you and, if not stopped, destroy you.

Is there any sin worth facing these consequences? No. But few people stop and think about where sin will take them. They feel good when they are with the "person of their dreams." One thing leads to another, and before they know it, their passions are out of control and the very thing that God has given us to experience in love and joy becomes tragic and destructive.

One reason people are so free with sex is that they don't want anyone telling them what to do, especially God. They don't want to read what He says about sin in the Bible, and they don't want to know about the consequences of sin. Sometimes, in the aftermath, someone will say, "If I had only known then what I know now."

Well, you can know. The author of Proverbs told us to keep our eyes set on God:

> Let your eyes look directly ahead
> And let your gaze be fixed straight in front of you.
> Watch the path of your feet

And all your ways will be established.
Do not turn to the right nor to the left;
Turn your foot from evil. (Prov. 4:25–27)

THERE IS HOPE

How do you turn a wayward life around once you have given yourself to sin?

First, acknowledge that what you have done is not right. This may mean going through some very lean weeks, months, and perhaps years before you actually say, "This is not God's best for me."

Once they have been blinded by sin, many people will not accept the truth about their circumstances. Their lives are spiraling out of control, yet they continue to prop up the ends and sides, hoping something will change. It never does when sin is involved.

Without a doubt, there will come a day when they run out of excuses. All the denial they have maintained will be filled with holes, and they will admit the bitterness and disappointment in their lives. This is when they will confess their sin to God. Confession is the starting point to healing and wholeness. You do not have to wait years to say, "God, please forgive me for what I have done—for opening my heart to sin and desiring the very thing that You have warned me to avoid."

The moment you pray and seek His forgiveness, He will draw near to you. In times of repentance, you agree with Him that your actions and attitudes were wrong and that you are willing to turn away from sin. This is what repentance is all about. We turn away from the sin that has caused a separation from God, but we also turn toward Him, acknowledging our need for Him and His truth.

Second, take responsibility for your actions. This could include asking another person or persons to forgive you. It also means accepting that you were wrong and there is no one to blame but yourself. We make choices each day, and some can lead to deadly mistakes. For example, a woman may choose to dress seductively at the office or around her neighbor. Before long, she has drawn the attention of several men. It is not long before one or more make an advance toward her. She is married, and she knows when she puts on a low-cut sweater that she is playing with fire, but she ignores the warning.

The same is true for men: be sure that you are honest with yourself. Inviting temptation into your life is like walking blindly through a minefield. Recently, a married man decided to call a former girlfriend on the telephone just to talk. He wanted to clear up a misunderstanding that had taken place in their relationship years earlier. The problem was he was now married. After talking a few minutes, he told himself that what he had to say needed to be done in person. Therefore, he suggested that the two meet just to discuss the issue. This was a very wrong move on his part. If you trip the wire, you can expect an explosion. Thankfully, a friend intervened and asked the man to pray about what he was about to do. He did, and he realized his motives were not completely pure. He needed to take responsibility for what he had done, and he needed to begin by asking God to forgive him for inviting sin into his life.

God is faithful, and He will send a check into our spirits if we are about to do something that is not in keeping with His truth and will. If we ignore it, He may persist. However, He may also allow us to reap what we sow to show us the devastating effects of sin.

Third, be genuine in your repentance. Often people say, "I'm sorry," but they really want to say, "I'm sorry I got caught." If this is what you have done in the past, then you need to know that while family and friends may have been deceived, God wasn't, nor will He be in the future. He knows your heart inside and out. He knows what motivated you, and He sees everything you do and knows what you are going to do before you take the first step. He will not tolerate sin. He may allow it to continue for a season, but sooner or later, you will have a day of reckoning.

Fourth, ask God to help you forgive yourself. Once you have come to the end of yourself, ask God to restore your fellowship with Him. After yielding to sin with Bathsheba, David prayed,

> Be gracious to me, O God, according to Your lovingkindness;
> According to the greatness of Your compassion blot out my
>   transgressions.
> Wash me thoroughly from my iniquity
> And cleanse me from my sin.
> For I know my transgressions,
> And my sin is ever before me.
> Against You, You only, I have sinned
> And done what is evil in Your sight. . . .
> Purify me with hyssop, and I shall be clean;
> Wash me, and I shall be whiter than snow. (Ps. 51:1–4, 7)

David's words reflect true repentance and godly regret. They also contain a remarkable sense of faith in a loving God who always restores and forgives sin. David knew there was only one place where he could find the forgiveness that his soul needed and craved, and it was in the presence of the living God.

NO MORE RUNNING

When some people talk about the sin that is consuming their lives, they speak of how they cannot be still. They spend their lives rushing and running from what seems to be an unseen phantom. It is not a phantom that is stalking them. It is the Spirit of God seeking to convict them of their sin.

You do not have to run another day. Starting this moment, you can begin to experience genuine peace and security through faith in Jesus Christ. I have talked to countless people who cannot seem to come to grips with this one area. Their minds tell them that they are healthy and normal people. While they are not married, they contend that they have sexual needs that must be answered. My answer is the same: "No, you don't."

This is not a trite answer. God has promised to meet every one of our needs. He is not going to satisfy one need and let the others go. Likewise, He is aware of your inner desires. These often fan the flame to sexual sins: "My desires. My needs. My determination, regardless of the consequences." That was David's position, and it led to the deaths of two sons and ultimately his downfall as king. Actually, his sin set the stage for the division of Israel and their later captivity. Never tell yourself that what you are doing will never hurt someone else. It will. The ripple effect of sin goes on and on.

Satan knows that sexual sin, like nothing else, has the ability to destroy the inner fabric of our faith in God. However, the Lord always promises to meet our needs in this area. This may not come in a physical form, but when we tell him the battle we are facing, He will raise up a standard of hope and help on our behalf.

God has the ability to defuse any type of sinful passion and replace it with a sense of godly contentment. Many people say, "There is no way God can meet all my needs, especially in this area." Oh, yes, there is. He knows the way to bring fulfillment apart from sin, but you must trust Him and learn to be still in His presence—not agitated and fretful because you want something He has forbidden.

If you will allow Him to have control of your sexual desire, He will show you how to live with a pure heart, whether you are married or single. Like most spiritual battles we face, overcoming sexual temptation requires a committed faith in God—one that acknowledges His sovereign care and goodness.

ELEVEN

THE LANDMINE OF SLOTHFULNESS

The young worker looked across the counter in the restaurant where he was working. His face was emotionless, and it stayed that way as he listened to the woman explain how every coffee carafe on the coffee bar was either empty or contained cold coffee.

Although I don't drink coffee, I can imagine that unless it is a planned drink, ice-cold coffee could taste awful, especially when the person is expecting a steaming, hot beverage.

The worker never offered to rectify the situation. After the woman talked for a few minutes, he simply shrugged his shoulders, walked over to one of the coffeemakers, and said, "I really don't drink coffee." To the woman's amazement, instead of making a carafe of fresh coffee, the young worker went back to his cash register and waited on the next person in line.

A LANDMINE THAT ROBS US OF PURPOSE AND MOTIVATION

Slothfulness or laziness is inexcusable. Usually the person who struggles with this landmine also exhibits signs of much deeper problems—low self-esteem, pride, and a passive-aggressive attitude. In 2 Thessalonians, Paul wrote to a group of believers who had become lazy in their devotion to God and in their work. Before you hesitate to read further because you think this may not apply to your life, ask yourself, *Am I doing my best?* or *Do I offer something much less to my employer and coworkers as a result of taking shortcuts and procrastinating?*

Many of the Thessalonians were not working. Instead, they expected the church to take care of them. When Paul got word of their dismal state, he penned two letters that contained strong words of admonishment, telling them that while Jesus had not returned, God was indeed faithful to His promises. The Savior would return. Therefore, until He did, they were to remain diligent in every area. That meant going back to work! But laziness is not confined to the area of employment. We can become lazy or slothful in relationships, our approach to life, and even how we deal with problems.

Paul wrote, "Now we command you, brethren, in the name of our Lord Jesus Christ, that you keep away from every brother who leads an unruly life and not according to the tradition which you received from us" (2 Thess. 3:6). Once the apostle began to address the struggling New Testament community, he went straight to the heart of the issue. He didn't mince words, and neither should we when we are dealing with the enemy. Satan truly believes that if he can entice us to step off the path God has for us, then we will trip a landmine, and the explosion that follows with be strong enough to harm us deeply. Attitudes of laziness can be very difficult to overcome because they involve motivation. A lazy person usually is someone who has given up trying. He becomes convinced that he does not have what it takes to make it—in relationships, on the job, or in society. So, he becomes lazy and allows others to go before him.

The lame man at the pool of Bethesda is a perfect example. John provides an account of this man's life,

> Now there is in Jerusalem by the sheep gate a pool, which is called in Hebrew Bethesda, having five porticoes. In these lay a multitude of those who were sick, blind, lame, and withered, waiting for the moving of the waters; for an angel of the Lord went down at certain seasons into the pool and stirred up the water; whoever then first, after the stirring up of the water, stepped in was made well from whatever disease with which he was afflicted. A man was there who had been ill for thirty-eight years. When Jesus saw him lying there, and knew that he had already been a long time in that condition, He said to him, "Do you wish to get well?"
>
> The sick man answered Him, "Sir, I have no man to put me into the pool when the water is stirred up, but while I am coming, another steps down before me." Jesus said to him, "Get up, pick up your pallet and walk." Immediately the man became well, and picked up his pallet and began to walk (John 5:2–9).

Christ's question, "Do you wish to get well?" is an important one, because many who gathered at the pool had no real desire to be healed. They made a handsome living begging for alms. It seems that if he had truly wanted to be healed, he would have positioned himself closer to the water. Instead, he had spent many years lingering along the sidelines of life. Perhaps he had given up and gave in to the idea of slothfulness.

Jesus always calls the lazy person into action. Paul directed the Thessalonians to go back to work, and the Lord called this man to get up and walk. Every landmine we face can be overcome, but not on our own. We need the Lord's help, guidance, and strength. We also need His foresight. He knows what is up ahead in life. We may think we can take time off and just drift for a while, but we can't. Once when I was a teenager, a friend and I went hiking through the woods near my hometown. We walked down to a nearby river and spotted an abandoned boat. We thought it would be fun to drift down the river. For a time, this is exactly what we did. It wasn't long until we heard a very loud roaring sound and knew we were headed for a waterfall. My friend looked across the boat and said, "Charles, I can't swim!" Suddenly, life turned very frightening. Since we did not have any oars with us, we had to get out of the boat. I was able to pull us over to the shoreline, but I remember thinking as I watched the boat go over the edge of the falls that this could have been a very costly price to pay for a lazy afternoon of drifting.

The Thessalonians had become discouraged, and many wanted to give up and quit. Instead of going to the Lord in prayer, the believers became perplexed, worried, angry, disobedient, and careless. They also allowed their lives to become lazy. They knew God's truth but had stopped living for Him. If we are not careful, we can fall into this same trap. Paul told them,

> For you yourselves know how you ought to follow our example, because we did not act in an undisciplined manner among you, nor did we eat anyone's bread without paying for it, but with labor and hardship we kept working night and day so that we would not be a burden to any of you; not because we do not have the right to this, but in order to offer ourselves as a model for you, so that you would follow our example.
>
> For even when we were with you, we used to give you this order: if anyone is not willing to work, then he is not to eat, either. For we hear that some among you are leading an undisciplined life, doing no work at all, but acting like busybodies. Now such persons we command and exhort in the Lord Jesus Christ to work in quiet fashion and eat their own bread. But as for you, brethren, do not grow weary of doing good. (2 Thess. 3:7–13)

CLEAR GUIDANCE

The Bible is very clear about the landmine of slothfulness. It results from a temptation that each one of us will face more than once.

Perhaps we have been through a series of disappointments, and our current challenge seems to be more than we can bear. We quickly discover that the enemy is relentless. He tells us that what we are facing is much too hard for us. We must stop, lean back, and drop out of life.

That was exactly what the Thessalonians did. They stopped working and believing in God's promises. They also became very lazy. In his letter to them, Paul issued one set of instructions: don't abandon your faith, and get back to work! God wants us to look our best and do our best at all times. This does not mean that we will be perfect or that our lives and work will be error-free. It does mean that we can try to do the very best that we know how to do.

During your lifetime, you will make mistakes. Plus, your best may not look like that of someone else. Never compare what you do to others. God knows your limitations, and He also knows what you are capable of achieving. The enemy, however, wants you to fail. One way he gains your attention is by telling you that you will never be as good as someone else. Don't believe it, and don't fall victim to his chatter. He would love for you to stop working and become ineffective in your witness for Christ.

All of us know people who are lazy and seem to be floundering professionally and personally. They really do not contribute to society, but they are the first ones to line up for a handout. They have ability, but they don't want to use it. From God's perspective, this is sin.

The young man at the coffee shop probably did not like his job. Chances are, he won't keep it very long. But if his employer should fire him, I wonder what Satan's message to him would contain. "You really don't need a job like this," or "You are worthless anyway. It was just a matter of time before you failed." The enemy lures us into thoughts of failure and then spends a lot of time and energy tempting us to feel horrible about ourselves.

Instead of viewing life in light of God's Word and truth, this young worker was looking for an easy way out of doing work, and he chose to do nothing.

In Proverbs 20:4 we read, "The sluggard does not plow after the autumn, / So he begs during the harvest and has nothing." In other words, a person who wants to be diligent must learn to think the way God thinks. This includes coming to a point where you understand that if you are going to have something in life, you must be willing to invest time and effort.

AN EXTREME DANGER

The motto of a slothful person is: "Don't do today what you can put off until tomorrow." He is not motivated to work or to try to do his best. Often he will procrastinate and refuse to accept any responsibility.

This type of person may start well but never finishes what he begins. Laziness takes over. It becomes a lifestyle that is very hard to break. Deep inside, the lazy person may want to achieve great things but cannot find the right amount of energy or determination needed for the challenge.

If you think you are on the verge of becoming lazy, you need to think about your situation and how the lack of motivation will prevent you from enjoying the very things God has given you. As with other struggles, you must make a conscious choice to go forward by faith and not be pulled down by Satan's desire to prevent you from living life to the fullest.

Some people have abandoned any hope of reaching their full potential. Countless talented but lazy people seek government aid every year. They are trapped in a cul-de-sac of slothful thinking that includes disappointment, low self-esteem, and a victim mentality.

Certainly there are times when a person has few options, if any. One trial after another may have left an individual fighting to keep food on the family's table. I am not talking about this kind of situation. I am addressing the person who knows God has given him truth, talent, and the ability to earn an honest day's wage, yet he refuses to do it. Or the little he does undercuts the grace and mercy of a loving God.

You may be down to your last dime, or you have just spent your last dollar for a basic need. Fear has gripped your heart as you wonder what you will do next. Seeking social aid is acceptable, but I would encourage you never to allow this to become a lifestyle. God has given you gifts and talents He wants to use for His glory. For years, my mother worked in a textile mill. She never complained about the long hours or the poor working conditions. I was always proud of her. She worked because she had a dream that was greater than our daily problems as a family struggling to make ends meet. She believed God had something better in mind for me and for her. Therefore, she also had a grateful heart. When people came to visit, she always found something to offer them. It was never much, but it taught me a principle that I will not forget: never focus on the difficulty of your circumstances; instead, focus on God, His faithfulness, and His resources, and be grateful for what He has given.

Mother had an amazing ability to see beyond our trials to a place of provision. We may not have had much, but what we had was enough. God was enough, and He used those early years of my life to mold my faith in Him. If my mother had said, "I'm not going to do this anymore. I'm tired and worn out. We're going to take handouts from others and get by some way," my life would have been filled with worry and fear. I never would have believed it was possible to come through the storms of life victoriously.

She never said anything like that. She got up very early and went to work. In doing so, she taught me a life principle, and that was to be responsible and do what God has given me to do for a season of time. I never heard my mother ask God why we did not have more. He always provided for every need we had, and He also proved His faithfulness over and over again.

The message we send our children is extremely important. If you are content lying back and allowing others to support you without your lifting a finger to work, then you are telling your children it is okay to be lazy. They will grow up lazy, and even worse they will grow up not knowing the potential within their lives.

God created each one of us for a purpose. When we live in slothfulness, we miss doing His will because we are engulfed by selfish thoughts and longings that will never come true.

There is no way the young man in the coffee shop felt good about his attitude. He may have grown up in a family where this type of lifestyle was modeled for him. Or at some point, he may have gained attention through being lazy. Some people need attention so badly that they will take negative attention, believing it is better than nothing.

A slothful person makes up his mind that he does not want to do something, and then he finds a way not to do it. This is a dangerous position.

You may be working in an organization that has demanded more of you than you can deliver. Emotionally you are drained. One day you wake up and think, *I'm just not going to do that anymore.*

You don't talk about your decision with God. You just decide you are going to check out mentally and physically. You may get away with this attitude for a while, but sooner or later, you will experience disappointment greater than what you did on your job.

After all, you think, *it is my life. I can do what I want to do.* But really you can't. By deciding that you will do nothing, you have placed even greater limitations on yourself. And if you do not stop the downward spiral, you will be even more frustrated.

THINGS TO CONSIDER

God expects us to live disciplined lives. A successful baseball pitcher never learns to throw searing strikes by giving up on the game. Instead, he spends hours every day practicing—throwing balls and then watching videos of his performance as well as the performance of others. He is diligent, and he is determined.

To defeat laziness, we must be committed to the task and to God. People who achieve success have several things in common: ability, commitment, discipline, desire, and a stick-to-it attitude. They do not give up when life becomes difficult—and it always does.

From another perspective, you may be an heir to a Fortune 500 company. You spend your weeks traveling or drifting over the links of some of the top golf courses in the world. You think you have it made, but you don't.

To succeed, you will need to work even harder than the fellow in the office cube on the bottom floor of the company that one day you will run. The reason is simple. The Bible tells us: "From everyone who has been given much, much will be required; and to whom they entrusted much, of him they will ask all the more" (Luke 12:48).

Your family connection may place you in a position of importance, but if you are lazy, profits will decline and stockholders will demand your resignation. Like the other sins discussed in this book, laziness of heart and mind isolates us from situations where we can do our greatest work. This also prevents us from achieving goals and learning even more about life.

The young man described at the beginning of this chapter has an opportunity to do well on his job. However, with his current attitude, he probably will end up quitting and moving from one job to another, complaining that conditions are not right or that he is being treated poorly.

When we think about the men and women in the Bible, we discover that each one of them confronted tremendous challenges. Joseph was sold into slavery in Egypt. He ended up becoming a servant in Pharaoh's household and later was accused of something he did not do. In the beginning, Joseph's life was a recording of one injustice after another. However, he did not allow his circumstances to hold him back from being the best he could be.

He worked hard, even in prison, and won the attention of the chief jailer. Soon he was in charge of the other prisoners. Have you ever thought about the fact that God is trying to teach you something through your circumstances? He is. He is in the process of training you for a greater work. However, the very thing that can derail His efforts is an attitude of slothfulness.

Proverbs 6:9–11 asks,

> How long will you lie down, O sluggard?
> When will you arise from your sleep?
> "A little sleep, a little slumber,
> A little folding of the hands to rest"—
> Your poverty will come in like a vagabond.

As I have said before, there are continuing consequences of sin.

Remember, a spiritual landmine is something each one of us will face—sometimes daily, if not hourly. You may think, *I don't feel like helping out. I don't want to go down to the second floor and work stuffing envelopes. That's not my job.* Sooner or later your despondent attitude will be noticed, and you will have no one to blame but yourself for the outcome.

My mom did not give up because she had a goal, and that was to help me to grow up to be the best I could be. She also had learned the principle of giving God the very best she could offer.

We can never outgive God. People who are financially lazy miss a tremendous blessing. They overlook the fact that everything they have was given to them by God. All that they hope to receive in the future is a result of His blessings in their lives.

Laziness can create an atmosphere of ingratitude. It also can promote an attitude of greed. Our world spends far too much time focusing on what people have rather than on what is important. Money will not make you a better person. It may open certain doors, but it will never bring deep satisfaction.

You can have more than you will ever use and still be lonely. Some of the richest people in the world are also the loneliest. True contentment and joy can be found only in a personal relationship with the Savior. And for this, you will need to be committed to Someone and something other than the idea of laziness.

LAZINESS AND YOUR EMOTIONS

People can also become emotionally lazy. They may have discovered through an early illness or some trauma that they could gain attention by appearing to be weak. They have never grown up or invested the time to become disciplined. They do enough work to get by but constantly seek to get others to make up for their deficiency. As seen earlier in Proverbs 20:4, "The sluggard does not plow after the autumn. So he begs during the harvest and has nothing." Do you really want to live life as a slothful person who does not work but ends up begging from others?

What are some of the characteristics of laziness?

Lack of priorities, goals, and ambition. The lazy person will not set goals, because he has no desire to reach them. He lacks ambition and does just enough to get by.

Selfishness. Laziness by nature is a very selfish attitude. The lazy person is consumed with his needs and little else. The nightly news is filled with reports of child abuse where mothers have left children at home alone without a second thought of how they would survive.

One mother recently left her children in the care of a friend who became tired of babysitting and also left. Three days later the mother returned from serving time in jail only to find that her daughter was in a diabetic coma and her son had not eaten in days. Careless, thoughtless actions carry with them tremendous consequences—if not for us, certainly for those around us.

Lack of faith in God's call and ability. Laziness leads to a faithless lifestyle. The person who has entered this lifestyle may profess to be a believer, but there is no evidence of faith. If there were, he would want to trust God for something better in the future. There is a sense of deadness in the heart and soul of the lazy person that is hard to understand.

The only way to describe it is to think of it in light of what the person is missing. It is void of true hope, commitment, and faith. Laziness robs us of God's greatest gifts—the ones that He brings and allows us to open with joy and hope for the future.

A sense of pride. In the beginning of this book, we discovered that pride was a foundational struggle for everyone. We will be tempted to become lazy, but when this happens, we need to realize pride is at work in our hearts. Proverbs 26:12 poses this question: "Do you see a man wise in his own eyes? / There is more hope for a fool than for him." Pride can prevent us from honestly working and being the best that we can be. It causes us to be lazy in our motives. We may allow others to do the work we should be doing because we believe the task is beneath us or we just don't have the time to give to certain situations. We forget that Jesus came to earth to serve and not to be served. His life is an awesome example of discipline and humility.

Pride steals the pure joy God wants us to experience. It blinds us to things that truly have value and tempts us to chase windswept dreams that are empty and full of sorrow. Nothing is more sorrowful than a person who is lazy and has little to no ambition. It is a mark of selfish pride because laziness has no interest in pleasing God.

Insensitivity to the Lord and to others. "Me, myself, and I" is the only motto a lazy person knows.

Unfinished tasks. A person who struggles with a slothful attitude will have a hard time finishing what he begins. His manager may assign a project to him, but weeks later, the paper for the job is hidden under mounds of other papers on his desk. He may have started an outline or put up the framework, but he will never finish what he began.

Sometimes this may happen when a person does not believe in himself. He may listen to the enemy's lie that tells him that he does not have what it takes to do the task. When God calls you to do a job, He assumes responsibility to equip you for the task.

A lazy person gives up. However, a person who is determined to do what God has given him to do will pray for help and wisdom for the project.

A damaged testimony for God. Believers have a keen responsibility to be energetic and committed. Laziness does not fit who we are in Christ. Jesus rested, and there will be times when we need to do the same. But He never withdrew from His earthly ministry for the sole purpose of escaping responsibility.

Weakened relationship with God. When you become lazy in one area, you will be slothful in other areas. In fact, every area will suffer, especially your worship and devotion to God. Lazy people do not think about pleasing the Lord; they think about how little they can do.

Ignorance of the truth. Once we know and understand God's truth, we are without excuse. A person who is not committed to Christ will avoid reading and studying Scripture. The enemy tells him it requires too much effort. He can go to church and hear a nice sermon, and that is all he needs to do. Laziness in our devotion to God is the most deadly because it leads to compromise, a void of truth, and spiritual ignorance.

If we fail to spend time with the Lord in prayer, we will not know just how much He loves and cares for us. We will never mature spiritually or have the tools to combat the negative rebuttals of the enemy. When it comes to prayer, many well-meaning Christians mistakenly think they can take time off. But they are opening a broad door to temptation and spiritual failure.

While there may be times when you don't spend as much time in prayer, it is deadly to think you can take a vacation from God. Satan never takes any vacation time, and if you become lazy, he will make sure to take full advantage of your laxness.

Feelings of depression, anxiety, and fear. Laziness never motivates a person to read more Scripture. Instead, it shouts, "Whew, you have done enough. Just drop back and rest." The enemy knows that when you become lazy, you also will grow slack in devotion to God.

When you forgo reading His Word, you will not have the spiritual tools to stand against such feelings as anxiety, depression, and low self-esteem. The truth of God's Word is our greatest spiritual weapon. It is our only offensive weapon against Satan's arsenal of negative, slothful words.

As I mentioned much earlier, the apostle Paul instructed us to

be strong in the Lord and in the strength of His might. Put on the full armor of God, so that you will be able to stand firm against the schemes of the devil. For our struggle is not against flesh and blood, but against the rulers, against the powers, against the world forces of this darkness, against the spiritual forces of wickedness in the heavenly places. Therefore, take up the full armor of God, so that you will be able to resist in the evil day, and having done everything, to stand firm.

Stand firm therefore, having girded your loins with truth, and having put on the breastplate of righteousness, and having shod your feet with the preparation of the gospel of peace; in addition to all, taking up the shield of faith with which you will be able to extinguish all the flaming arrows of the evil one. And take the helmet of salvation, and the sword of the Spirit, which is the word of God. With all prayer and petition pray at all times in the Spirit, and with this in view, be on the alert. (Eph. 6:10–18)

Peter also admonished us, "Be of sober spirit, be on the alert. Your adversary, the devil, prowls around like a roaring lion, seeking someone to devour. But resist him, firm in your faith" (1 Peter 5:8–9).

Satan is always on the move, looking for places to hide his landmines. He wants to trick you into doubting, ignoring, and rebelling against God's will and purpose. Laziness is just one of his wicked tactics. If you give this struggle room to grow in your heart, you will face

- *problems.* These may include the loss of a job, a relationship, or internal peace.

- *stress and pressure.* Laziness is a doorway to procrastination, which brings stress. Employers and friends don't want to be the ones to carry us through life. Sooner, rather than later, most people get tired of a lazy person's attitude.

- *emotional as well as physical pain.* If you are going to be lazy, you probably will have to grow accustomed to settling for last place. A lazy person is not necessarily looking to come in first place. Often we see this in the arena of sports or on our jobs where we settle for doing just enough to get by.

- *a lack of peace.* Your heart will be troubled, because deep down inside, every person wants to know she counts for something. Anxiety and a sense of dread will loom over a person who is entrapped in slothful living.

- *poverty.* When you don't work, you can't eat. Or maybe you eat because someone else is paying your bills. The reality is that you miss God's blessing—trusting Him to provide for all your needs. A lazy person may say, "Well, this is what I am doing," but James reminded us that the evidence of faith is our desire to work and be excellent in all that we do. When we do this, we honor God. We glorify Him with our actions, and He makes up for any lack we have.

- *penalty.* We always reap what we sow, more than we sow, and later than we sow.

OVERCOMING THE LANDMINE OF LAZINESS

You do not have to fall victim to any of Satan's schemes. Both Peter and Paul provided insight into combating the enemy and the struggle of laziness. You can overcome this problem when you understand the following:

God has created you for a purpose. He loves you, and if you will trust Him, He will set up the circumstances so that you can enjoy every moment.

You are not powerless. A spirit of laziness will tempt you to think you will never be free. However, God's Word tells us that through the death of His Son, you can have freedom and power over every single form of bondage. Freedom is gained through faith in His Son.

Jesus tells us, "If you hold to my teaching, you are really my disciples. Then you will know the truth, and the truth will set you free" (John 8:31–32 NIV). Once you accept Christ as your Savior, His Spirit—the Holy Spirit—comes to abide with you. There is no greater power available than the power God's Spirit provides. However, you must appropriate His strength to your life.

God has a plan for your life. In Jeremiah 29:11, He assures us: "'I know the plans that I have for you,' declares the LORD, 'plans for welfare and not for calamity to give you a future and a hope.'"

If you allow laziness to establish a stronghold in your life, you will never realize the hope and the many promises that are yours in Christ. God wants us to trust Him so He can bless us, but this very fact is based on our faith in Him. Will you trust Him enough to get up and walk toward Him, believing that He wants to give you a future that is more than you dreamed possible?

Lazy people wait for someone or something to drop into their lives.

They want an easy ride with no form of commitment. But true joy comes when we decide to take God's challenge and begin a walk of faith with Him.

God forgives sin. God stands ready to forgive your sin and to give you the wisdom and strength to overcome this struggle with slothfulness or any other sin. However, you must seek His forgiveness and also confess where you have been lazy and careless, beginning with your love and devotion for Him. You also must make a choice to turn away from sin. In the case of laziness, it may take all the effort you can manage because the enemy will not let go of you easily.

You are in spiritual warfare, but there is no need for you to lose this battle. When your faith is firm in Christ, He will fight for you and provide a way out of this bondage.

He is your only source of victory. Life's greatest foe is no match for God's Son. He is your victory, your hope, your defender, your stronghold, your strength, and your fortress (Ps. 18). He is also your deliverer, who sets you free from the bondage of sin. He has overcome the world, its passions, lusts, and fears. More important, He has overcome the enemy. Satan is a defeated foe. You do not have to take one single step toward any of his landmines.

When you pray, ask God to give you His discernment and wisdom, not only for your present circumstances but also for every area of life. You will face times of temptation—all of us do. But you have the ability through Jesus Christ to discern right from wrong, godly behavior from sinfulness. You will never go wrong obeying God and following His pathway of righteousness. Satan's destructive devices will no longer be a threat.

One day, Jesus will return for those who know Him as Savior and Lord. When He does, you will see Him face-to-face and know the fullness of His eternal joy. All of life's battles will end, and the goodness of God's love will be yours for eternity!

TWELVE

DEFUSING THE LANDMINES ALONG YOUR PATH

God gave Abraham and Sarah an awesome promise—one that would change their lives and one that demanded extreme trust. They would have a son, even though they were far beyond childbearing age. Sarah was tempted to compromise her faith in God. After hearing the Lord's promise, she laughed (Gen. 18:13). And God noticed the laughter and asked, "Is anything too difficult for the LORD?" (v. 14). Jeremiah echoed these same words: "Lord GOD! Behold, You have made the heavens and the earth by Your great power and by Your outstretched arm! Nothing is too difficult for You" (Jer. 32:17).

Many times we launch out on our own and end up stepping on a landmine because we fail to consider God's might and powerful love for us. We don't take time to think about His personal promises. Instead, we mentally rush past evidences of His faithfulness; dismiss His ability to heal, provide, and restore; and move forward without consulting Him about the future. When we make a conscious decision to bypass God and His principles, we make a horrendous mistake. "I couldn't help myself," one man, who was involved in a relationship with a woman other than his wife, told me. He was a believer, but he stepped on the landmine of sexual sin and suddenly his life changed—not for the better.

"Oh, yes, you could," I replied. "You have the ability to say no because Jesus Christ lives within you through the presence of the Holy Spirit."

One of the greatest mistakes believers make, especially when it comes to the subject of sin and particularly the landmines, is a lack of faith. Without a strong faith in God, we will become easy targets for the enemy. Like Sarah, we will be tempted to laugh instead of obey. Proverbs 3:5–7 gives us a simple principle but one that we can use to avoid the trappings of Satan:

> Trust in the LORD with all your heart
> And do not lean on your own understanding.
> In all your ways acknowledge Him,
> And He will make your paths straight.
> Do not be wise in your own eyes;
> Fear the LORD and turn away from evil.

The way to avoid a landmine is to stay close to the One who has promised to guide you safely through the danger.

"If only I had known, I never would have gone to the party. I'm so sorry." The words fell from the teenager's mouth with unbelievable regret. However, nothing he offered could bring back his friend who had been killed as a result of his drunk driving. People fail to heed God's warnings because ultimately they do not know how deadly a landmine can be. They ignore the fact that they are responsible to God for their actions. A single sin—such as the sin of compromise—can lead to a number of other problems, such as gossip, doubt, and even feelings of anxiety. When our lives are not firmly attached to God, then trouble is sure to come. The same is true of every landmine on our list. For example, the landmine of fear can paralyze us and even tempt us to become jealous of others who are not entrapped by feelings of worry, dread, and panic. These are just two examples.

Every landmine poses a serious threat to the path of the believer. Unbelievers are not affected because they have never accepted Christ as their Savior. Their lives are one huge explosion. There is nothing more devastating than living your entire life apart from God's love.

GAINING AN ETERNAL PERSPECTIVE

A believer's battlefield is marked with stations of victory. Not every day will be a struggle. Not every trial will seem insurmountable. God has given us the eternal victory, and we can say with the apostle Paul, "In the last days difficult times will come. . . . I have fought the good fight, I have finished the course, I have kept the faith; in the future there is laid up for me the crown of righteousness, which the Lord, the righteous Judge, will award to me on that day; and not only to me, but also to all who have loved His appearing" (2 Tim. 3:1; 4:7–8). Even when he faced extreme trials, Paul had an eternal perspective. But there is no way a lost person can feel this same way because he has chosen to walk straight onto the battlefield with no way of detecting the landmines hidden just below the surface of his life.

Set off one landmine and a series of explosions can occur quickly. For example, the enemy may gain access into your life through a certain area, such as the landmine of unforgiveness, but his overarching plan is to trick you into compromising your faith and distancing yourself from God. He will stop at nothing to achieve this goal. The reason? He knows that if he can get you into a place of spiritual ineffectiveness, you will no longer be in a position where God can use you. He wants to find a way to keep you from loving God and experiencing His love in return. To be loved is the greatest need we have. To be loved unconditionally is the gift that God extends to everyone who accepts His Son by faith. However, to experience this close, intimate relationship, you must be willing to draw near to Him through personal surrender and submission.

This is where the rub usually takes place. Many people do not want to bow their knees to God, and they walk away from Him without a second thought about where the path they are on will take them. You can go to church every Sunday and still end up hitting a landmine if your life is not submitted to God. Living for Christ involves a heart commitment and not just a personal performance. There will be times when you run up on a landmine, and it explodes beneath you. This is exactly what happened to Peter on the night of Christ's arrest. At one point, he promised the Lord that he would never betray him. He cringed at the sound of the Lord's words telling him that on that very night he would turn away. Peter, like most of us, did not want to believe the obvious, which revealed his vulnerability to enemy attack.

In *My Utmost for His Highest,* Oswald Chambers writes, "There is only one relationship that matters, and that is your personal relationship to a personal Redeemer and Lord. Let everything else go, but maintain that at all costs, and God will fulfill His purpose through your life. . . . Always remain alert to the fact that where one man has gone back is exactly where anyone may go back. . . . Kept by the power of God—this is the only safety."

God wants to use the brokenness we experience in the aftermath of a landmine explosion. After His resurrection, He made a point to reinstate Peter and even commissioned him for greater service, and this is what He wants to do in our lives. If a landmine had the power to completely destroy a child of God, then it would have more energy and more velocity than God. But it doesn't. God is omniscient, omnipresent, and omnipotent. Absolutely nothing is greater than our God.

There are two ways we encounter landmines. *The first is by taking a route that God does not want us to travel without knowing the consequences.* Many times, we make mistakes. We may sense God warning us to be careful and not take a wrong step, but we do it anyway, thinking that maybe we will be okay. When the explosion occurs, we immediately turn to the Lord and seek His forgiveness. His grace sufficiently covers us in such times. We may still have to experience the consequences of our sin, but we also will have a deep sense of peace within our hearts because we have acknowledged our wrong choice and asked Him to lead us back to safety.

The second is by making a choice without any consideration of God. In other words, we know there are consequences. However, our passion and desire to reach our own goals supersede what we know is right. Sarah laughed because she was being cynical, not because she thought God was funny. If she had thought about what she was doing in the presence of God, the only action she would have taken would have been to fall down on her face in worship. The same is true for each one of us. Every day we make countless choices—some include important decisions, while others on a human scale may seem minor.

From God's perspective, some of the smallest decisions are the most important because they reveal our true nature and character. This is why you should tell the clerk at the store when he gives you too much change. And it is exactly what our children and peers need to witness overflowing from our lives—a desire to be godly and avoid landmines, even the small ones that can be just as deadly as the large ones. If we say one thing but act in another way, we send the wrong message to those around us. And while some may not know the truth, God does, and one day He will ask us to give an account for the times that we have chosen a path that leads straight to harm and danger.

GOD WANTS TO PROTECT YOU

Our military has a new armored blast-resistant vehicle that will withstand a direct hit from an enemy landmine and protect those riding within it. It is called the Cougar, and it is on the battlefield right now in limited numbers. But more are on their way. Another vehicle named the Buffalo, which is being used to clear roadways of dangerous landmines, also employs the same design and technology. What is the secret to the success of these "gold standard vehicles of choice"? The answer is found in the pronounced V-shaped steel hull, which forces the blast out and away from the vehicle.

One soldier told how a roadside bomb went off under the rear of the Cougar in which he was riding, and he did not even know it had been detonated. "The only way we knew we had been hit was because we heard radio chatter," he said.

At times, you may wonder whether there is a safe way to cross the minefield that the enemy has laid out in front of you. The answer is yes. You do not have to become a victim of his deadly arsenal. God is willing to protect you, but He can't do this if you are determined to cross the minefield without His protection. Even in times when you have openly embraced a danger with destructive potential, He is willing to intervene on your behalf, but you must turn to Him in prayer and express your need and desire to walk rightly before Him.

Each day, you face a minefield, but even when an explosion does take place, God is willing to disperse the intensity of the blast. Another important step you can take in clearing the minefield of dangerous weapons is exposure—but not to Satan's ploys. Instead, open your heart to God and ask Him to search the landscape of your life and reveal anything to you that is not in keeping with His best. Then you will be on the road to victory. The truth is, your life has a built-in V-shaped hull because His Spirit lives within you as a child of God.

Even though you may choose to sin or step away from His will, His love covers you (1 Peter 4:8). He does not agree with or support your sinful actions, but He never stops loving you. And when you turn back to Him, He forgives and restores the relationship you share with Him as your Savior, Lord, and loving heavenly Father. Just as the Cougar's V-shaped hull sends the force of a landmine's blast out and away from the armored vehicle, God's forgiveness will redirect the enemy's potentially deadly blast in your life.

In Psalm 139, David wrote,

> Search me, O God, and know my heart;
> Try me and know my anxious thoughts;
> And see if there be any hurtful way in me,
> And lead me in the everlasting way. (vv. 23–24)

David's humility was evidence of his desire to strip away anything that would separate him from the Lord. His words also reveal the heart of a man who had learned to avoid many spiritual dangers.

David was proactive. He wanted to know God and His ways.

He had a submissive spirit. He did not have his own agenda in mind but actually wanted to please God above all else.

His life was open to God. David was willing for God to "try" him to see if he had learned what he needed to know. People ask me, "How can I avoid sin?" There will be times when we grapple with severe temptation and trial. Sometimes this comes as a result of sin, and other times it comes as a part of living in a fallen world. Landmines can explode in either case. I may experience a season of difficulty that leaves me struggling financially. However, I feel victorious until I look at a friend who seems to have much more than I have, and envy and jealousy begin to build. Still, I must make a choice to narrow my focus to the problem and the landmine or turn to God, confessing my weaknesses and seeking His help and strength. If I make the second choice, then I will gain victory. If I take a direct hit from a landmine, I must admit where I have gone wrong and ask God to help me get back on track.

David wanted God's will for his life. He prayed, "Lead me in the everlasting way" (Ps. 139:24). He had an unquenchable desire to know God. When this is the goal of your heart, an alarm inside you will go off, and you will want to go in another direction as you approach a landmine. One woman was recounting how she had been in an extremely stressful environment on her job. She became so tired that she began to ignore God's Spirit. In conversation, she sensed Him telling her not to repeat something she had heard in an earlier conversation. But she did not listen. Other times, she admitted that she felt as though God did not want her to do a certain activity, but once again, she did not listen. She said, "I even got to a point where I would say, 'Lord, I know You have said not to do this, but I'm going to do it anyway.'"

Each time she made this type of conscious choice, she was getting closer to stepping on a landmine, but she did not stop. Finally, she ended up losing her job and struggling with depression. In the aftermath of this horrendous explosion, God gained her attention. When He says stop, we need to listen if for no other reason than who is doing the talking.

GOD'S PRESENCE: A PLACE OF EXTREME CARE

Years ago, I found myself in a very trying set of circumstances. But, the Lord made it clear that He wanted me right where I was. There was no question about it. Even though I faced opposition, I had to remain focused in my walk with Him. Each day, I found myself down on my face before God, praying for insight into the battle raging around me. There was never a doubt in my mind that God would work everything out, but I did wonder how He would do this. Still, I was committed to staying steadfast.

Often God will allow our faith to be stretched in ways we did not think we could bear. Each time a trial comes or increases in intensity, we are stretched a little further. In the process, God is strengthening our faith, building our trust in Him, and teaching us to watch for His direction. Whenever I felt overwhelmed by my circumstances, I reminded the Lord that I was not going to move an inch without His direct guidance. The more time passed, the more committed I became. Any thought of launching out where I could be in danger of stepping on a landmine faded. And the Lord gave me a wonderful verse of Scripture to claim for my situation. It was Isaiah 54:17:

"No weapon that is formed against you will prosper;
And every tongue that accuses you in judgment you will condemn.
This is the heritage of the servants of the LORD,
And their vindication is from Me," declares the LORD.

When you are facing a very difficult situation—one that would tempt you to get off the course God has planned for your life—the most powerful thing you can do is to go to God's Word and pray, "Lord, point me to the anchor that I need from Your Word." There is one thing about an anchor; it never moves. The anchor that holds fast within our hearts is our relationship with Jesus Christ. He is immovable and unshakable. When He gives you a promise of hope, you can cling to it, knowing that He is going to protect you and work in your life in an amazing way. This is exactly what God did in my life. He turned my circumstances around, and I did not have to lift one finger in an effort to alter my situation. The victory was awesome because it belonged to Him and not to me.

Now you know what landmines are, where they are located, and how to avoid them, the question you will have to answer is, how will you handle them? Do you ask God to help you avoid them so that you do not have to be devastated by their blast? The psalmist wrote,

The steps of a man are established by the LORD,
And He delights in his way.
When he falls, he will not be hurled headlong,
Because the LORD is the One who holds his hand. (Ps. 37:23–24)

THE FAITHFULNESS OF GOD

God is the One who walks with you through each day. The road you are on does not have to lead to an intense combat zone. As a believer, you will undergo many trials and disappointments, but you can learn to spot the landmines that the enemy places along your way and avoid serious injury. In the process, you will gain a depth of intimacy with God that you cannot gain any other way. There is something deeply moving about being on the battlefield with Him where there is no way of safe escape except to find cover in His sheltering arms. David learned there was only one place of extreme safety, and that was in God's extreme care.

Will you trust Him to order the steps of your life, to lead you along a pathway that is secure from enemy attack, and to grant you a genuine peace that cannot be stripped away by anything this world throws at you? When you do, you will be amazed at the peace you feel inside. Even though there will be occasions where you face serious temptation, you will not fall as long as you are holding God's hand.

He wants to give your life meaning, hope, and purpose. He knows all the times you have failed, and He still loves you and will forgive you when you turn to Him and ask for His forgiveness. He will take you from where you are to where you need to be. He knows exactly how to get you on the right path—the one that is landmine-free. In the process, He will satisfy the deepest longing of your heart. He will never disappoint you because He always chooses the best for you to enjoy. He has a fantastic plan waiting for you. It does not matter if you are six or ninety-six. The moment you say, "Lord, use me, train me, and teach me more about Yourself," He will answer your prayer, and all of heaven's joy, contentment, and eternal peace will be yours forever.

Do you ever wish you could have more of In Touch at your fingertips?

Dr. Stanley and In Touch Ministries are just a click away. Find exactly what you need faster and easier than ever before at *InTouch.org*.

Log on now to:

- Watch and listen to Dr. Stanley's messages.
- Read daily devotions and inspiring articles from *In Touch* magazine.
- Get answers to your questions about God.
- Download In Touch Podcasts.
- Support In Touch by donating online.
- Discover how to have a life full of joy and purpose.
- Shop at the easy-to-use online bookstore.
- Find strength to help you through difficult times.
- See how In Touch is reaching people around the world.
- Learn how you can make a difference in your own home and community.
- Enjoy special online offers.

In Touch's mission is to lead people worldwide into a growing relationship with Jesus Christ and to strengthen the local church. Whether you're a new believer or a mature Christian, InTouch.org can help you draw closer to God. Log on to *InTouch.org* today and take advantage of all the great things In Touch Ministries has to offer.